# The BIG Book of
# STRESS-RELIEF
# GAMES

Other books in *The Big Book of Business Games* series are:

*The Big Book of Business Games*
*The Big Book of Creativity Games* (also by Robert Epstein)
*The Big Book of Customer Service Training Games*
*The Big Book of Flip Charts*
*The Big Book of Humorous Training Games*
*The Big Book of Presentation Games*
*The Big Book of Sales Games*
*The Big Book of Team Building Games*

# The BIG Book of
# STRESS-RELIEF GAMES

## Quick, Fun Activities
## for Feeling Better

**Robert Epstein, Ph.D.**

Editor-in-Chief, *Psychology Today*
University Research Professor, United States International University
Director Emeritus, Cambridge Center for Behavioral Studies
Chairman and CEO, InnoGen International

**McGraw-Hill**

New York  San Fransicso  Washington, D.C.  Auckland  Bogotá
Caracas  Lisbon  London  Madrid  Mexico City  Milan
Montreal  New Delhi  San Juan  Singapore
Sydney  Tokyo  Toronto

## McGraw-Hill

*A Division of The* **McGraw·Hill** *Companies*

    4 5 6 7 8 9 0   AGM / AGM   0 9 8 7 6 5 4 3 2

ISBN 0-07-021866-8

*The sponsoring editor for this book was Richard Narramore, the editing supervisor was Paul R. Sobel, and the production supervisor was Charles Annis. This book was set in Arial by Jessica Rogers. Printed and bound by Quebecor / Martinsburg.*

McGraw-Hill books are available at special quantity discounts to use as premiums and sales promotions, or for use in corporate training programs. For more information, please write to the Director of Special Sales, McGraw-Hill, 2 Penn Plaza, New York, NY 10121-2298. Or contact your local bookstore.

This book is printed on recycled, acid-free paper containing a minimum of 50% recycled de-inked fiber.

To Elva Becerra,
stress-free mom,
for breakthroughs
and more.

# CONTENTS

# ACKNOWLEDGMENTS

My longtime editor at McGraw-Hill, Richard Narramore, coached me through the preparation of the book with his usual patience and proficiency, performing relaxation exercises all the while. Hara Estroff Marano and Lyle M. Spencer, Jr. helped, in one way and another, to set the book in motion. Art Robin introduced me to "The Turtle Technique." Both Julian Reyes Epstein and Alberta Swett pointed out the surprise in the word "desserts." Heather Bennett, Espen Correll, Allison Gill-Hooten, and Michelle Osborne, helped research some of the techniques. Saba Varghai, a student at the University of California San Diego, helped with the proofreading. I'm especially grateful to Jessica Rogers, an editorial intern at *Psychology Today* magazine and a student at United States International University, for her tireless help in preparing the manuscript.

# The BIG Book of

# STRESS-RELIEF

# GAMES

# getting

# ready...

# INTRODUCTION TO
# STRESS MANAGEMENT

"Desserts" spelled backwards reads: *"Stressed."*

Life is like that. It seems that almost everything we do, even many of the fun things, have the potential to make us feel bad. Go to work—stress. Go home—more stress. Eat a piece of chocolate cake—hey, why not just put down the fork and put a gun to your head?

This book is a remedy for our desserts-rich, stressed-out lives. In the pages that follow, you'll learn just about every major technique that's ever been developed for managing stress, and you'll learn these techniques in a stress-free way—through fun, quick, easy-to-play games.

Want to learn meditation but haven't got the time to spend six months in an ashram in India? Try "Meditation for the Impatient" (page 99). Want to escape from your office for a few minutes to visit the make-believe world of the Beatles' "Lucy in the Sky with Diamonds"? Try "Tangerine Trees" (page 147). Want to learn a powerful, stress-relieving breathing technique while singing the theme to the Popeye cartoon show? Try "Popeye Puffs" (page 113). Want to learn how to handle rude, arrogant, inconsiderate neighbors or supervisors? *Definitely* try "The *Whoosh* Game" (page 187).

Get the idea? This is a collection of unique games that teach a wide range of techniques for managing stress—while you and the members of your group (or your supervisees, or your students, or your children) have fun.

# Dire Need

You need this book. Why? Because the world is full of alligators, they're creeping up on you from every side, and your defenses are weak. And this applies to just about everyone you know. We're all trained as children in the basics of reading and basketball, but we're taught *nothing* about stress management. As adults, we flock to therapists or physicians or gurus or yoga classes or health clubs, anxiously seeking magic cures for the stress we feel, but relief rarely comes, and it's usually just temporary.

Read the stats: Close to *90 percent* of visits to primary care physicians are for stress-related problems. Nearly *750,000* Americans attempt suicide each year, often because of unmanageable stress. On an average work day, about *a million* employees are absent because of stress-related problems. Job stress costs American businesses more than *$200 billion dollars a year* in absenteeism, worker compensation claims, health insurance costs, and lowered productivity. *Forty percent* of employee turnover is stress related.

Stress tears our bodies apart. Recent studies show that stress weakens our immune systems, increases the risk of heart disease, impairs mood and performance, disturbs our sleep, contributes to sexual dysfunction, destroys relationships, and generally makes us miserable. (See the overhead on page 12 to see just how miserable.)

Stress *management* either *protects* you from stress ("proactive" stress management) or *reduces* stress levels ("reactive" stress management), resulting in enormous benefits for health, mood, performance, relationships, and organizations. (See the overhead on page 13 to see just how good things can be.)

# The Games and Their Uses

This book contains fifty fun activities that teach just about every kind of stress-management technique that's ever been tested, included some (like relaxation postures—see "Ready, Set, Sit!" page 123) that are fairly new. I've included *imagery* games (both "guided" and "unguided" imagery), *muscle-relaxation* games, *stretching* games, *thought-restructuring* games, *breathing* games, and even games that help you distinguish good stress-management techniques from bad ones (see "The Good, the Bad, and the Ugly," page 63).

The games are arranged alphabetically by title, and I've tried to create titles that are upbeat and memorable.

You can use this book in several different ways. If you have the time to read through the book, simply jot down the names of the games that seem most appropriate for you and your specific training needs.

Don't feel like training anyone? No problem. I've added a "Personal Touch" section to many of the games which explains how to use the technique to manage your own stress. In other words, this book will help you if you're a leader or teacher, and you can also use it for personal growth.

Here are few common training situations, along with games I think are especially useful for such situations. Keep in mind that your own situation might require a different mix.

> *Loosening up an audience:* "Gravity Magic" (page 67), "Punch that Pillow! (page 115), "Reach for the Sky" (page 119), "Warmth of the Sun" (page 177).

*Teaching people to cope with interpersonal conflict:* "Beliefs That Can Kill" (page 23), "A Little Help from My Friends" (page 89), "Make Me Laugh" (page 93), "The Time-Tested Ten Count" (page 161), "The Whoosh Game" (page 187), "The World Is Round" (page 195).

*Reducing staff stress:* "The Beastly Boss Game" (page 21), "Compu-Relaxation" (page 41), "The Laugh Graph" (page 85), "Punch That Pillow!" (page 115), "Stacked to the Ceiling" (page 139), "The Twenty-Eight-Hour Day" (page 173), "What D'Ya Know?" (page 181), "The Whoosh Game" (page 187), "The World Is Round" (page 195).

*Activities for people in a rush:* "Blowing Away the Tension" (page 29), "The Make-a-Fist Technique" (page 91), "Meditation for the Impatient" (page 99), "Popeye Puffs" (page 113), "Ready, Set, Sit!" (page 123), "The Terrific Tummy Technique" (page 155), "The Whoosh Game" (page 187).

Note that a single game might be useful for a number of different training situations.

If your focus is on *skills* rather than *situations*, you'll want to select the games in a different way. For example, if you'd like people to strengthen *proactive* stress-management skills—skills that protect people from possible sources of stress—you may want to use games like: "The Beastly Boss Game" (page 21), "Building a Relaxation Machine" (page 35), "The Good, the Bad, and the Ugly" (page 63), "Keeping the Fires Burning" (page 79), "The Nirvana Room" (page 103), "Ready, Set, Sit!" (page 123), "Red, White, and Very Blue" (page 127), "The Ten-Year Planner" (page 151), "The Twenty-Eight- Hour Day" (page 173), "What D'Ya Know?" (page 181), or "The World Is Round" (page 195).

If you want your students to strengthen their *reactive* stress-management skills, you might want to use games like: "Blowing Away the Tension" (page 29), "Punch That Pillow! (page 115), or "The Time-Tested Ten Count" (page 161).

In general, there are four different types of stress-management "competencies" (more on that below). If you're trying to train specific competencies, pick your games appropriately.

## Stress: Lose It, Don't "Use" It

Most people think the concept of psychological stress is an ancient one. Not so. It was invented by researcher Hans Selye in 1936. Selye showed, mainly in rats, that the body reacts to a wide variety of demanding situations in roughly the same way: with higher blood pressure, tense muscles, dilated pupils, increased hormonal activity, and so on. In effect, the body is getting ready to meet the new demand—to attack or run away from a predator, for example. Unfortunately, if the body is kept in this heightened state for too long, both the immune system and the vital organs begin to deteriorate.

Selye distinguished between *stress*, a state of the body, and *stressors*, the external demands. You'll find up-to-date definitions of "stress" and "stressor" in the overhead on page 11.

There's something curious about the relationship between stress and stressors: *You can feel stress in the absence of a stressor, and a stressor might not produce stress!* In other words, stress and stressors don't necessarily go hand in hand.

And that is the key to stress management.

If you believe the world is flat (see "The World Is Round," page 195), you might panic when you see a boat go over the horizon, imagining that everyone aboard is drowning. In other words, even *imaginary threats* can produce real stress. How you *interpret* or *perceive* a situation is critical. Interpret things one way and you'll feel stress; interpret things a different way, and you'll feel fine.

Similarly, you might be surrounded by real threats and feel perfectly calm. Surrounded by lions, most people would be terrified, but an experienced lion tamer might feel perfectly in control.

The skills and beliefs you carry with you into a situation determine whether or not you'll experience stress in that situation. Skills can be improved, beliefs can be modified, and situations can be altered—all of which means that you have the power to "manage stress."

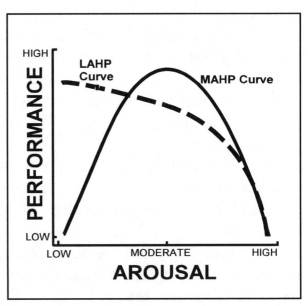

*Figure 1.* "Map vs. "Lap": According to the traditional MAHP Model ("Moderate-Arousal High-Performance"), peak performance is achieved when we're moderately stressed. A more contemporary perspective, called the LAHP Model ("Low-Arousal High-Performance") suggests that with skillful stress management, we can achieve peak performance under very low levels of stress.

Selye and others believed that stress could be a good thing—that we could learn how to handle stress in a positive way. Some have even taught that a moderate state of arousal is *necessary* for peak performance (*Figure 1*).

But the state of arousal associated with stress is destructive if maintained too long, and it's possible to perform well over a wide range of arousal states. Writers often can write only when they're completely at peace, and soldiers often perform great feats under extremely high states of arousal. Averaged, these peak states might make a moderate state of arousal look best, but the *healthiest* combination is the one in which you perform well without stress (*see Figure 1*).

# Getting Serious:
# Building Stress-Management Competencies

There are four different types of skills or "competencies" that one can develop to manage stress:

1) *Source management:* The individual reduces or eliminates sources of stress.
2) *Relaxation:* The individual practices relaxation techniques on a regular basis.
3) *Thought management:* The individual manages his or her thoughts to reduce stress.
4) *Planning and analysis:* The individual plans for the future, avoids destructive methods of stress management, and uses proactive methods of stress management.

You'll find more information about these categories in "What D'Ya Know?" (page 181), along with a short quiz that determines how strong someone's skills are in each area.

The quiz is a shortened version of the *Epstein Stress Management Inventory for Individuals (ESMI-i)*, which is marketed by InnoGen International (www.innogen.com or 1-877-INNOGEN). A related test, the *ESMI-m*, measures a manager's ability to minimize employee stress.

Notice that these types of tests don't measure a person's *level* of stress. That kind of measure can be pretty discouraging, and it often leads to unflattering labels. A competency approach to stress management is more positive and constructive. It simply indicates how strong one's skills are in certain areas. With appropriate training and practice, the skills improve.

If you need more detailed versions of the games in this book, consult *Stress-Management and Relaxation Activities for Trainers* (McGraw-Hill, 1999).

Meanwhile, when surrounded by alligators, befuddle them with Popeye puffs, tell them a good joke about alligator shoes, picture yourself in a boat on a river, and, above all, remember that the world is round. It is, you know.

**STRESS**: a state of physiological imbalance in the body which has unpleasant emotional and cognitive components.


**STRESSOR**: something that threatens your safety or well-being.


Do STRESSORS necessarily produce STRESS?

Is all STRESS necessarily produced by STRESSORS?

# COSTS OF STRESS

- Weakened immune system
- Increased risk of disease
- Increased blood pressure
- Increased risk of heart attack and stroke
- Increased vulnerability to cancer
- Poor mood
- Slower healing
- Permanent or long-term damage to the brain
- Impaired memory and thinking
- Menstrual difficulties
- Pregnancy difficulties
- Sleep disturbances
- Relationship problems
- Sexual dysfunction
- Absenteeism
- Lowered productivity
- Increased cost of health insurance
- Increased compensation claims

# BENEFITS OF
# STRESS MANAGEMENT

- Strengthened immune system
- Reduced risk of disease
- Decreased risk of heart attack and stroke
- Improved mood
- Improved memory and thinking
- Increased productivity
- Improved sleep
- Improved relationships
- Improved sexual performance
- Reduced absenteeism
- Steadier insurance costs
- Reduced compensation claims
- Improved morale
- Improved workplace environment
- Increased company loyalty

# the
# games!

# THE ANTI-BOREDOM GAME

## In a Nutshell

Participants learn how to use slow periods wisely by imagining a state of boredom and then exploring the emotions associated with that state.

## Time

10 minutes.

## What You'll Need

Writing materials for every participant, copies of the overheads on pages 19-20, and a timer or clock.

## What to Do

Ask participants to do absolutely nothing for 2 minutes. Tell them that for the next painful  minutes, you want them to feel bored.

Observe the participants while you're timing the exercise.  Announce the time every 15 seconds, and make your announcements sound dull and flat.  When the time is up, ask a few people to tell the group, in as much detail as they can, how they actually felt.

Briefly review some of the basic characteristics of boredom and two strategies for beating boredom, using overheads on pages 19-20.

## Discussion Questions

1) How can a lack of demands cause stress?
2. How can repetitious tasks cause stress?
3. What methods do you currently use to fight boredom?
4. What other methods might you use?

## If You Have More Time

Divide the groups into Mutual Support Teams (see page 89) of between three and five people. Have everyone write a brief description of a work situation he or she finds boring. Then give the team members 10 minutes to help each other create Anti-Boredom Plans for eliminating the boredom.

## Personal Touch

To fight boredom in your own life, put yourself through the exercise. Then list "inward" and "outward" techniques that you can use to add more stimulation and challenge to your routine (see the overhead on page 20).

# SOURCES
# OF BOREDOM

- A LACK OF DEMANDS
- REPETITIOUS TASKS

# CHARACTERISTICS
# OF BOREDOM

- FEELINGS OF HOSTILITY
- URGE TO ESCAPE
- RESTLESS LIMBS
- LOW PRODUCTIVITY
- URGE TO MOVE AROUND
- RUMINATIVE THOUGHTS

# BEATING BOREDOM

- **FOCUSING INWARD**
  **Walking, Jogging, Stretching**
  **Daydreaming, Visualizing**
  **Relaxing, Planning**
  **Skill-Building**

- **FOCUSING OUTWARD**
  **Seeking More**
  **Responsibility,**
  **Seeking Promotion,**
  **Seeking a New Job**

# THE BEASTLY BOSS GAME

## In a Nutshell

This game helps participants learn and practice skills to help control their anger when faced with an insensitive manager or supervisor. Participants role-play scenes in which a manager or supervisor acts insensitively, during which they practice simple breathing or imagery techniques to help them stay calm and respond constructively.

## Time

10-15 minutes.

## What You'll Need

Writing materials for each participant.

## What to Do

For 4 or 5 minutes, lead everyone in the room in a few simple breathing and imagery exercises (such as abdominal breathing). Now, distribute prepared role-playing scenes or have each participant describe a scene on paper. Next, put people into pairs. Ask one person in each pair to be the Beastly Boss and the other to be the Exemplary Employee. Exemplary Employees should, *as inconspicuously as possible*, practice one or more breathing or imagery techniques during the scene. Have them spend two or three minutes acting out the scene.

Following the role plays, lead the group in a discussion about the effects that the relaxation exercises had on their interactions and, especially, on the *outcomes* of the interactions.

## Discussion Questions

1. How realistic was your role play? How was it like the real situation, and how was it different?
2. Were you able to practice your relaxation techniques during your play? If not, why not?
3. What are the pros and cons of venting your anger with your boss?
4. Why should you practice these techniques *inconspicuously* during workplace interactions?

## If You Have More Time

Have people perform the role plays first before you introduce the relaxation techniques. Then teach the relaxation techniques, have people switch roles, and have them act out the scenes again while the Exemplary Employee performs a relaxation exercise. Ask people from each pair to report on the differences in the two plays.

# BELIEFS THAT CAN KILL

## In a Nutshell

After presenting the participants with some common examples of irrational beliefs, they'll make their own lists of irrational beliefs that may underlie some of the stress they feel on the job.

## Time

15-20 minutes.

## What You'll Need

Writing materials for all participants, copies of the handout on page 25, and a flipchart, blackboard, or overhead projector.

## What to Do

Identify some beliefs that are "irrational" and then discuss this concept with the group. Review the handout on page 25 for ideas. Then explain how irrational thoughts can lead to stress, and elicit reactions and suggestions from the group on this topic. For example, if someone believes that everyone else at work is incompetent, how might his or her behavior be affected?  How might interactions with others be affected?  How might feelings of stress be produced?

Introduce the idea of Substitute Rational Beliefs, or SRBs.  With the group, generate some SRBs that correspond to a few of the irrational beliefs previously discussed.

For example, if someone believes that he or she is always late, an SRB might be: *I'm late for appointments two or three times a week, which is more often than I'd like.*

Finally, display a list of irrational beliefs, and ask participants to propose Substitute Rational Beliefs.

## Discussion Questions

1. How can irrational beliefs hurt you?
2. Is it possible to harbor irrational beliefs that can actually *reduce* stress or help you in some other way?
3. How does one go about abandoning irrational beliefs?

## If You Have More Time

Have the participants write down three of their own irrational beliefs, and have them generate one or more SRB for each irrational belief.  Ask a few people to share what they have written, and lead a discussion about these examples.

## IRRATIONAL BELIEFS

I'm always late.
I can't do  anything right.
Everyone around me is incompetent.
I'll never get ahead  in this job.
I always do my best.


## SUBSTITUTE RATIONAL BELIEFS

I'm often late.
I do some things right but not others.
Each of my co-workers has strengths and
   weaknesses.
I need to find new strategies for
   advancement.
I perform well in many situations.

# THE BLISS LIST

## In a Nutshell

Participants create and post their own lists of relaxing and stress-reducing activities to make it more likely that they'll engage in such activities during the day.

## Time

15-20 minutes.

## What You'll Need

Writing materials, and a flipchart or blackboard.

## What to Do

Remind the participants that we often let days or weeks or months go by without doing any of the simple things that make us relax and allow us to manage daily stress. Tell them that one simple way to fight this tendency is to create and post a Bliss List—a list of activities that make you feel great.

Have participants spend a few minutes listing as many relaxing activities as they can.

Finally, ask people to make a written commitment to post copies of their Bliss Lists in at least three specific places:

*I hereby commit to posting copies of my Bliss List in all of the places I've listed above, with the intention of reminding myself to engage in as many of the listed activities as possible, as often as possible.*

_____
*Signature*

## Discussion Questions

1. Bliss Lists need to be updated from time to time. Why?
2. How can you make it more likely that you'll keep your List up-to-date?
3. Why is it important that Bliss Lists be posted and not simply written down?
4. How could you use your computer to post your Bliss List?

## Personal Touch

Sometimes stress hits home even worse than at work. Help beat stress by making your very own bliss list and posting it prominently.

# BLOWING AWAY
# THE TENSION

## In a Nutshell

Participants learn the "cleansing breath" and are taught ways they might use it during the day to combat stress.

## Time

5-10 minutes.

## What You'll Need

No special materials are needed in this exercise.

## What to Do

Explain the basics of the "cleansing breath." It might be helpful to describe each part of it before you proceed:

*First we're going to inhale very deeply–in fact, we're going to take a huge noisy breath in, exaggerating the effort. I'll demonstrate shortly. Second, we're going hold that breath to a slow count of five. And, finally–and this is the good part—we're going to let all of the air out very, very slowly, and, as we do so, we're going to blow away all of the tension in our bodies, until we've blown out all of the air.*

Now, demonstrate a cleansing breath.

Have the entire group practice the technique together, slowly and deliberately, two or three times.

Ask people how the cleansing breath makes them feel. Most people will report feeling very relaxed.

Now lead a discussion about how the cleansing breath might be used during the day to combat stress.

## Discussion Questions

1. Would you be reluctant to do a cleansing breath at work? Why or why not?
2. What are situations in which the cleansing breath might be useful for you? What are situations where you would be reluctant to use the cleansing breath?
3. What are advantages and disadvantages of the cleansing breath as a stress-management technique?

## If You Have More Time

Divide the group into small teams of between three and five people. Half the teams will have a "proactive stress" assignment, and the other half a "reactive stress" assignment. Each proactive team should decide on a single work situation in which the cleansing breath could be used for stress-proofing—fighting stress before it occurs. Each reactive team should decide on a single work situation that's extremely stressful and in which a cleansing breath could be used to shake off stress before it gets out of hand.

Finally, some of the groups should be called on to act out their stress scenario and show how the cleansing breath can be used in that scenario. The audience should be encouraged to react, comment, and have some fun.

## Personal Touch

The cleansing breath is also effective when you are at home. Let the deep, refreshing breath be part of your morning routine to prepare for the day ahead.

# BLOWING UP THE COMPANY

## In a Nutshell

Participants learn to use imagery and composition to reduce the anxiety associated with problems and challenges at work.

## Time

20-25 minutes.

## What You'll Need

Writing materials for each participant.

## What to Do

Explain to the participants that this exercise is based on a technique therapists call "flooding," in which you help someone overcome fear by having him or her imagine an extreme, almost absurdly fearful situation.

For example, if a woman is afraid of being criticized, you may have her imagine that a hundred people are standing around her in a circle, all shouting insults at her simultaneously. You might then have her imagine more extreme variants of this situation. Perhaps the shouts grow louder until the building begins to shake and the walls fall down. Then the shouts stimulate a massive earthquake, until the whole city is in ruins. These fantasies often end with the world blowing up in a puff of smoke. They make one lowly criticism seem pretty small and insignificant. In other words, they put things back into reasonable perspective. After all, many of the challenges we face each day—although irritating—aren't really very important in the grand scheme of things.

Now, distribute writing materials, and have participants list three irritating problems or challenges they face at work. Then have them outline their blowup fantasies. Have participants close their eyes, focus on one of the fantasies, and imagine it unfolding in detail.

Have them imagine the real problem with which they started, while you coach them through a simple relaxation exercise (such as the cleansing breath or a muscle relaxation procedure). Finally, have people share some of the blow-up fantasies with the group.

## Discussion Questions

1. How can putting things in perspective help us fight stress?
2. Do you find yourself getting upset over small matters? When does this happen and why?
3. How can the blowup technique be used proactively? Reactively?

# BUILDING A RELAXATION MACHINE

## In a Nutshell

Participants are taught how to use common objects to help them perform a simple relaxation exercise.

## Time

5-10 minutes.

## What You'll Need

An assortment of four or five common objects that can be used to help people relax. Suggested: a small pillow, a piece of paper, a working clock that has a second hand, a pencil, a magazine photo of a tropical scene, and a red push-pin.

## What to Do

Show the participants some of the objects that you've brought with you, and engage the group in a discussion about how these items might be used to promote relaxation. For example:

*Pencil.*    Can be used as an aid in an eye-movement exercise.  Can also be used for drawing or scribbling.

*Magazine clipping of tropical scene.*  Can be used to launch a visualization exercise.

*Red push-pin.* Placed inconspicuously on the wall, this can be used as a "focus point" for imagery or breathing exercises.

## Discussion Questions

1. What objects, materials, and supplies are on hand in your work setting that could be used for relaxation?
2. What objects, materials, and supplies could be added to your work setting to promote relaxation?

## If You Have More Time

Here are some other objects that can used to help people relax:

*Small pillow.*  Can be placed on one's chair in the small of the back to help attain a more relaxed posture. Can also be placed on the floor to support the head, back, or knees during a breathing or visualization exercise.

*Blank piece of paper.*  Can be used to launch a visualization exercise, for drawing or scribbling, or as an aid in a simple meditation exercise.

*Clock with second hand.*  Can be used to time a relaxation exercise.  Focusing on one full cycle of the second hand can also serve as a simple form of meditation.

## Personal Touch

You can easily use all of the methods described in this chapter for your own stress management.

# CAPTURING A DAYDREAM

## In a Nutshell

Participants are asked to
close their eyes and let heir minds wander for a few
minutes and then to report both on their personal
experiences and on how they feel.

## Time

10 minutes.

## What You Need

No special materials are needed.

## What to Do

Give the participants permission to daydream for the
next few minutes. Advise them to sit in a relaxed
position and to close their eyes. Then walk them
through the exercise, as follows:

*Take a big breath in, hold it for a count of five, and
now, begin to exhale very slowly. As you exhale,
blow away all of the tension in your body. Now*

*breath normally and stay relaxed. All you have to do for the next few minutes is daydream. You may visit strange places. Just relax. Try not to control your thoughts. I'll ask you to open your eyes in a couple of minutes.*

After two or three minutes, have people open their eyes, and call on volunteers to report on what they experienced and how they felt.

## Discussion Questions

1. How do you feel after your daydream?
2. How can daydreaming have value for creativity? For relaxation?
3. When could a short daydream fit into your day?

## Tip!

Some people might be uptight about the idea of deliberately daydreaming at work. Tell them they've just mastered "Krishnamurti's Choiceless Awareness," a meditation technique that enhances productivity and creativity at work. They'll all want to join in!

## Personal Touch

Give yourself permission to daydream. Find times and places that make daydreaming easy, and let yourself go. Happy travels!

# COMPU-RELAXATION

## In a Nutshell

Participants learn about and design both feasible and futuristic ways in which technology can be used as stress-management and relaxation aids.

## Time

30-40 minutes.

## What You'll Need

Writing materials for the participants, and a flipchart, blackboard, or overhead projector for you. The handout on page 43 might be helpful.

## What to Do

Lead the group in a brief discussion about how computers might be used to aid in stress management and relaxation, both now and in the future. Jot down major category headings on your board or flipchart (see handout).

Then distribute the handout on page 43. Ask

participants, working in small teams, to spend about ten minutes completing the form you've distributed.

Finally, ask a representative from each group to present the ideas developed in his or her group, and lead a discussion about these ideas.

# Using the Computer to Relieve Workplace Stress
## Exercise: "Compu-Relaxation"

List specific ways that you might put the computer to use in your work or home environments to help relieve stress.  Some examples have been given to help give you a start.

---

*Screen Savers:*

    1.  Install soothing screen savers on all office computers.

    2.

    3.

    4.

*Games and Exercises:*

    1.  Obtain and use interactive muscle relaxation software.

    2.

    3.

    4.

*Internet Tools:*

    1.  Locate and use online counseling and emotional support services.

    2.

    3.

    4.

*Home Computer:*

    1.  Use the built-in CD player to play relaxation CDs while you work.

    2.

    3.

    4.

# CORPORATE SPACE ODDITY

## In a Nutshell

Participants relax while you talk them through a trip into deep space.

## Time

5 minutes.

## What You'll Need

No special materials are needed for this exercise.

## What to Do

Ask participants to get into a relaxed position, with their eyes closed. Next, take your participants on a journey in space by reciting the following text.

*Now that you're sitting comfortably, listen very carefully while I take you on a brief journey though space. Concentrate on my words and on my voice, just as you might have years ago when your mom or dad read you a bedtime story. Ready? Here we go...*

*You're feeling calm and comfortable. Focus for a moment on how your chair feels against your body.... Listen to yourself breathing in and out slowly, easily... You have a sense of anticipation, a sense that something wonderful is about to happen.... Now you begin to notice a feeling of lightness. Your body mass, your weight, is beginning to disappear. Your body is getting lighter and lighter, lighter than a feather, lighter than the air around you... You begin to rise off the seat of your chair. Slowly, very slowly, you're rising off of the seat of your chair. You feel so light, so happy, so relieved, as this happens. Slowly, very slowly, you continue to rise into the air. Your body is light and insubstantial, like that of a ghost. You continue to rise to the ceiling. Your body is so light and insubstantial that you pass right through the ceiling, right through the roof of the building, and into the air above. You feel peaceful and happy and contented as you continue to rise higher and higher, up into the air, faster and faster. The air feels warm around you, and you see buildings and cars and people below you, quickly receding as you move higher and higher. Finally, you rise above Earth's atmosphere, out into the beautiful blackness of space itself...*

*Below, you see the curve of the planet, brighter and bluer than you ever imagined it. You see the great oceans, and masses of brown land, and wisps of white clouds... You feel warm and safe and comfortable as you continue to gaze downward... The blackness of space itself envelopes your body. You look around and see thousands and thousands of brilliant specks of the bright light, all gleaming against the deep blackness of space... As you look around, you feel awed and exhilarated.... You never imagined that space could be so black, that stars could be so bright and abundant.*

*Now, slowly, gently, you begin to descend to Earth... Around you, as you enter the atmosphere, the blackness begins to fade to blue sky. Slowly, gently, you descend through the sky. Slowly, gently, you descend to your building. Slowly, gently, you descend through the roof, through the ceiling, into this room, into your chair.*

*You feel warm and comfortable and relaxed as you gradually... open your eyes....*

## Discussion Questions

1. How did the space fantasy make you feel?
2. How could you employ such an exercise during the work day?
3. What images might work well for you to help you relax during the day?

## Tip!

Your delivery is important here, and so is the environment. Try to keep your voice quiet and soothing as you take participants on their space journey. Distracting noises can spoil the journey for some people, so take care to close doors and windows before you start the exercise. You might want to record your voice (or perhaps someone else's) in advance of the session and then play the tape. You can even add soothing music.

## Personal Touch

Put the image text on tape for yourself, or have a friend recite the text on tape for you, perhaps with some soothing background music. Press play, close your eyes, and you're off.

# CORPORATE TELEPHONE

## In a Nutshell

Participants play two variations on the Telephone Game. One group passes a rumor from person to person without doing relaxation exercises. A second group does the same while doing relaxation exercises.

## Time

10 minutes.

## What You'll Need

Blackboard or flipchart.

## What to Do

Divide the audience into two groups. Have the first group relay an inflammatory rumor (that you supply) by whispering it from one person to the another. Simultaneously, have the second group relay the same rumor while participants focus on their breathing or, if you prefer, while they perform some other relaxation exercise.

Compare the final rumor in each group. Finally, lead a

**49**

discussion about the different outcomes of the two versions of the exercise.

## Discussion Questions

1. How is the Corporate Telephone game similar to real communication that occurs in the organizational environment?
2. How can stress lead to miscommunication? How can miscommunication lead to stress?

## Tip!

Make sure that your original rumors are somewhat complex and spicy! They're more likely to be distorted than simple, boring ones.

# THE CO-WORKER FROM HELL

## In a Nutshell

Participants role play scenes, either of their design or your design, in which they interact with difficult co-workers. They practice simple relaxation techniques during the interaction to learn to stay calm and constructive during the interaction.

## Time

30 minutes.

## What You'll Need

Writing materials for each participant.

## What to Do

First, distribute a prepared role-playing scene. To keep things simple, the scene should have a *Reasonable Rational Relater* and an *Irksome Irrational Irritant,* or, roughly speaking, a "Good Guy" and a "Bad Guy."

Next, put people into pairs, and have each pair spend two or three minutes acting out the scene, with one person being the Reasonable Rational Relater (RRR) and the other the Irksome Irrational Irritant (III). Next, for a few minutes, lead everyone in the room in a few simple breathing and imagery exercises.

Finally, have the pairs re-enact the scenes. This time, however, the RRRs should inconspicuously practice one or more breathing or imagery techniques during the scene.

Following the role plays, lead the group in a discussion about the effects that the relaxation exercises had on their interactions and, especially, on the *outcomes* of the interactions.

## Discussion Questions

1. How can relaxation techniques be used to improve the outcomes of interpersonal conflicts?
2. How realistic was your role play?
3. What was the outcome of your role play? How, if at all, did the relaxation techniques affect the course and outcome of the scene?

## If You're Short on Time

Put people in pairs, and have them act out a scene of your choice while one person practices a relaxation technique. Ask a few people to report on their experience.

# Alternative

Interpersonal conflict sometimes involves groups of three or more. You might want to try to work with larger groups to role play conflicts of this sort.

# DANCING WITH YOUR EYES

## In a Nutshell

Participants practice moving their eyes in a pattern that produces a relaxation response.

## Time

5 minutes.

## What You'll Need

No special materials are necessary.

## What to Do

Explain to participants that eye movement can be used to affect mood. Then, have participants sit in a relaxed position, and instruct them as follows:

*Slowly and easily, move your eyes upward toward the ceiling, as far as you can, and then downward toward the floor, as far as you can. Pause briefly at each extreme. Repeat this movement, slowly and smoothly and easily, ten times. When you're done, bring your eyes to the center position, looking straight ahead.... Now, slowly and easily, move your eyes all the way to your left, then all the way to your right. Repeat this movement, slowly and smoothly and easily, ten times, again pausing briefly at each extreme..... When you're done, once again bring your eyes center, and look straight ahead. Now, slowly and easily, move your eyes to the extreme upper-left corner of your field of vision, then in a straight line toward the lower-right corner of your field of vision, again pausing briefly at each extreme. Continue to move back and forth along this diagonal ten times.... Now repeat this movement along the other diagonal ten times, moving slowly and easily from the upper-right corner of your field of vision to the lower-left corner of your field of vision. Pause briefly at each extreme. Always move slowly and smoothly and easily, and remember to keep breathing.*

*Now, slowly and easily, move your eyes toward the ceiling again, and begin moving your eyes in a slow circle, clockwise, first down toward your right, then down toward the floor, then up toward your left, and up again toward the ceiling. Keep the movement slow and smooth and steady, and remember to keep breathing.... Now continue this movement until you've completed ten clockwise circles, and then bring your eyes back to the center position.... Finally, bring your eyes toward the ceiling once more. Now, slowly and easily, begin moving your eyes in a counterclockwise circle, first down to your left, then down toward the floor, then up to your right, then up toward the ceiling....*

*Continue this movement until you've completed ten counterclockwise circles.... When you're done, move your eyes back to center, and look straight ahead....*

Conclude the activity by asking a few participants to describe how they felt during the exercise and to say how they feel now.

## Discussion Questions

1. Did you feel any relaxation effect?
2. Do you think that eye movement can produce a relaxation effect? Why or why not?
3. How might you incorporate an eye-movement exercise into your daily routine?

## Personal Touch

You can practice this technique almost any time to help you relieve your own stress. If it helps, put the text on tape and play it when you need it.

# THE GLITTERING ROOF

## In a Nutshell

Participants imagine themselves sailing through the air over beautiful buildings, and they are transfixed by a glittering, sun-laden roof.

## Time

5 minutes.

## What You'll Need

No special materials are needed.

## What to Do

Ask participants to get into a relaxed position. Now have participants close their eyes, and take them on the following journey:

*Now that you're sitting comfortably, listen carefully while I help you develop a very beautiful, very relaxing image—in this case, a very simple one: the image of the sunlit roof of a very old house. Concentrate on my words and on my voice.... Ready? Here we go....*

*You're feeling calm and comfortable. Focus for a moment on how your chair feels against your body.... Listen to yourself breathing in and out slowly, easily.... You have a sense of anticipation, a sense that something wonderful is about to happen.... Your eyes are closed, but you feel the gentle rush of wind around you. You feel a cool, pleasant breeze caressing your face, your neck, your chest, your arms. You feel like you're moving forward through the air.... Keep your eyes closed, but imagine that your eyes are slowly starting to open. As you open your eyes, you see that you are gliding through the air over a beautiful old town—a town that seems to be in the English countryside, hundreds and hundreds of years old. As you continue to glide, you feel calm and peaceful. The breeze against your face is gentle and slightly cool. The small hairs on your skin tingle slightly as they are stroked by the breeze. You continue to glide forward, and you look around you, downward and to your sides.*

*Below you seek dozens of small homes. Cobblestone paths lead to each house. The roads between them are made of packed earth. You can see tracks along the roads where carriages have traveled. The roofs of the houses are a reddish brown. Here and there, between the houses, are old gnarled trees. The trees are mostly green, with a few yellow and reddish leaves on them. It's early autumn, and the colors are just about to change. The sun is low in the sky, and the trees and houses cast long gray shadows on the lawns and the roads....*

*You continue to glide, slowly, peacefully, feeling calm and secure.... Soon, up ahead you notice a larger building in the center of the village. Unlike the small homes around it, it seems to have two stories. It's made of old, weathered, oversized bricks, of yellow and red and brown, with generous lines of ancient mortar marking their boundaries. Perhaps it's the town hall, or perhaps it's an old library. As you near the building, you slow down, hovering above it....*

*The sun, behind you now and very low in the Western sky, is glittering off the old tiled roof of the quaint building beneath you. The sunlight is catching the tiles just right, so they seem to glow with warm reds and bright yellows and blues. As you shift position slightly in the air above the building, the colors shift and shimmer.... You're transfixed by the sight, feeling a sense of wonder and awe and harmony....*

*Gradually, very gradually, the sun sets behind you, and the image of the glittering roof begins to fade...to pale reds and yellows and blues...and then to soft shades of gray.*

*As you return to the present, the beautiful image of the glittering roof remains in your mind. You feel comforted and soothed by it. You feel at peace.... Now, slowly, open your eyes....*

## Discussion Questions

1. Were you distracted by our current setting? In what setting might this have been more effective for you?
2. How could you employ such an exercise during the work day?
3. What images might work well for you to help you relax during the day?

## Tip!

Try to keep your voice calm and soothing as you talk participants through the fantasy. In order to minimize distractions, close doors and windows before you start the exercise.

## Personal Touch

You can also fit this game into your personal stress-management regimen. Just record the text on tape, and play it whenever you need a quick get away.

# THE GOOD, THE BAD, AND THE UGLY

## In a Nutshell

Participants learn to appreciate the difference between constructive and destructive methods for managing stress.

## Time

15 minutes.

## What You'll Need

You'll need a blackboard or overhead projector on which to keep track of the techniques.

## What to Do

Ask participants to suggest as many techniques for managing stress as they can. When each new technique is suggested, have the audience shout either "Good!" or "Bad!," and write the technique in the appropriate column on the blackboard. For some or all of the techniques, ask people to justify each choice. Here are the kinds of lists you are likely to generate:

| *Good Techniques* | *Bad Techniques* |
|---|---|
| Popeye puffs (double blow) | Overeating |
| Cleansing breath | Too much chocolate |
| Swimming | Too much television |
| Jogging | Tranquilizers |
| Relaxation postures | Illegal drugs |
| Punching a pillow | Shouting at someone |
| Eye-movement techniques | Quitting your job |

## Discussion Questions

1. What's the difference between a good method for handling stress and a bad method for handling stress?
2. Why is it important to understand this distinction?
3. Why is it important to learn and master as many good methods as possible?

## Alternative

You may want to create a third list, called "Ugly Techniques." These are especially destructive methods for handling stress, which unfortunately, between 10 and 20 percent of the population resort to every day. Define "Ugly" techniques as ones for which the long-term consequences are life threatening. Substance abuse would fit in this category.

## If You're Short on Time

Display a scrambled list of good and bad techniques,

and ask people to help you sort them out.

## Tip!

By the way, "good" techniques produce only benefits, while bad ones tend to produce short-lived benefits (for example, a "high") followed by serious problems.

## Personal Touch

Make your own lists of the good and bad techniques you use to manage stress. Can you add more to the good list and eliminate some from the bad list?

# GRAVITY MAGIC

## In a Nutshell

Participants learn some simple "passive" stretches in which gravity is used to relax major muscle groups.

## Time

15-20 minutes.

## What You'll Need

No materials are needed.

## What to Do

Explain the difference between "active" and "passive" stretches. Roughly, in an active stretch, you tense one or more muscle groups in order to stretch and relax some other part of your body (see "Reach for the Sky," page 119). In a passive stretch, you allow gravity to bring about the stretch very slowly, further increasing the stretch by using breathing techniques.

Remind participants that with each exhalation, they should allow the stretch to increase slightly, relaxing that part of the body just a little more.

Almost any body part can be relaxed, at least somewhat, with a passive stretch. Some suggestions are shown on page 70.

## Discussion Questions

1. Will you be able to do passive stretches at work? Which ones are appropriate and which ones inappropriate for your work situation?
2. How can you use a simple breathing technique to increase a passive stretch?
3. Why do you think a stretch increases slightly when you exhale?

## If You Have More Time

Have volunteers, one by one, launch a projectile (such as a soft-tipped dart) at a body board (a diagram of a body). Use a spinner, and have each volunteer take a spin. Then ask for suggestions about how you might use gravity to stretch that part of the body. Guide the discussion until something practical emerges, and then lead the group in performing the stretch.

## Tip!

It's imperative that you emphasize throughout these exercises how important it is to come out of a passive stretch *slowly and easily*. Unlike active stretches, it's virtually impossible to strain yourself while performing a gravity stretch. You *can* injure yourself, however, while coming out of stretched position—whether achieved passively or actively—too abruptly.

## Personal Touch

The great thing about these stretches is that you can do them almost anywhere, almost anytime. Gravity stretches are quiet, non-taxing, and fairly quick. Doing them on a regular basis is an easy way to achieve a deeply relaxed state.

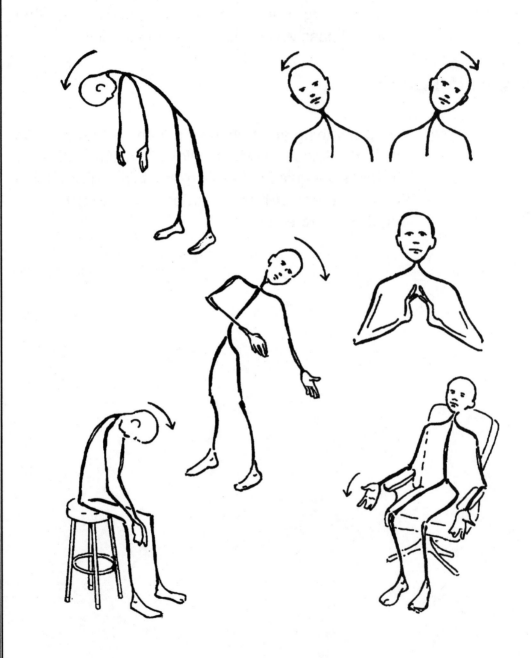

# HANDS THAT HEAL

## In a Nutshell

Participants are shown various self-massage techniques and asked to practice them.

## Time

10 minutes.

## What You'll Need

No special materials needed.

## What to Do

Demonstrate the self-massage techniques listed below and have people try them out. If you like, you can distribute copies of page 74, which outlines a two-minute self-massage regimen.

*Head.* Gently massage the head by moving the flats of your fingers in small circles against the skin. Start with the scalp, then move to the ears, the face, the forehead, and the temples. If you need to keep your hair in place, skip the scalp. Skip the face if you're wearing makeup.

*Neck and shoulders.* Continue the circular movements on the sides and back of the neck, and then on both shoulders.

*Feet.* If it's convenient for you to remove your shoes, use small circular movements of the flats of your fingers to massage your feet.

## Discussion Questions

1. What are the relaxation benefits of massage? What are other benefits?
2. Would it be possible for you to have occasional professional massages while in the workplace? What are the impediments?
3. What are the advantages and disadvantages of self-massage?

## If You Have More Time

Here are some other techniques you may wish to try:

*Arms.* Use circular movements at the joints, and use long back-and-forth movements up and down the long parts of each arm.

*Torso.* Use large, gentle circular motions against the front of the torso.

*Back.* Without straining, continue using large, gentle circular motions against whatever portions of your back you can reach.

# Personal Touch

Self-massage is also perfect *after* a long day at the office. Try these techniques after a nice, warm bath. Warm massage oils work wonders.

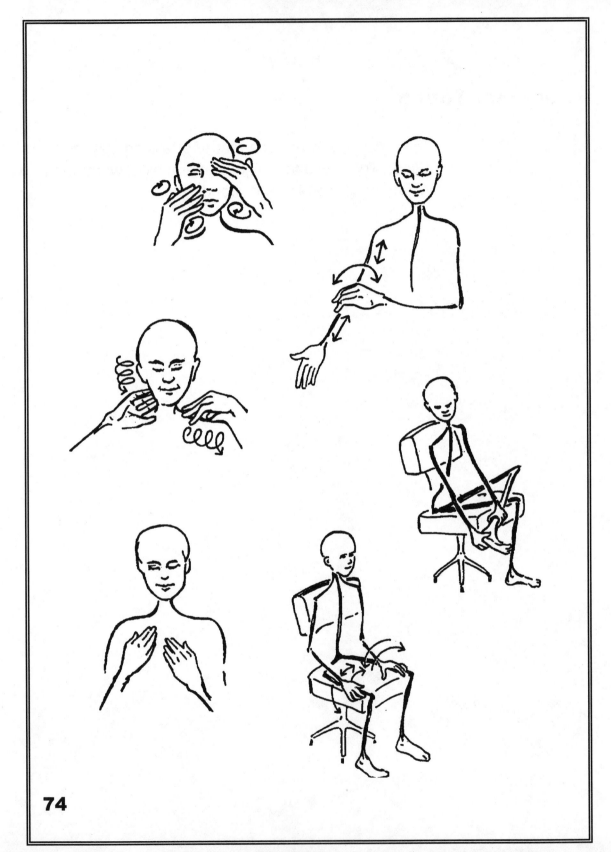

# HOUR POWER

## In a Nutshell

Using some simple self-management techniques, participants devise methods for making sure they take brief breaks from stressful or laborious tasks and routines.

## Time

15-20 minutes.

## What You'll Need

Writing materials for each participant.

## What to Do

Briefly review these categories, perhaps from a list you display on an overhead.

1) *Jumpers:* You have stacks of projects on your desk, and you spend hours jumping nervously from one to another. You feel completely exhausted when you finally stop working, and your stacks seem as high as ever.

2) *Diggers:* You work for long periods on a single project, never taking a break. You're exhausted when you stop, and you have some doubts about the quality of your work.

3) *Fidgeters:* You take far too many breaks. You're distracted by everything, even by particles of dust on the wall.

By a show of hands, see how many people you've got in each category. You'll probably have picked up more than three-quarters of the group. Ask a couple of the remaining people about their work patterns, just for contrast.

Explain that the work patterns of Jumpers, Diggers, and Fidgeters cause unnecessary stress. The best remedy for each of these patterns is to *schedule brief but frequent breaks.* Even a 30-second break can have dramatic benefits: It can *increase concentration, heighten creativity, reduce errors, boost efficiency,* and *relieve stress.* This is a good point to come up with examples of how you and others have gotten yourselves to take regular breaks. Now ask the members of your group to map out a personal strategy for break-taking.

## Discussion Questions

1. Are you a Jumper, a Digger, or a Fidgeter? If not, how would you describe your work pattern?

2. How, if at all, might you benefit by taking brief, frequent breaks from your work?
3. What techniques might you use to get more control over your pattern of working and taking breaks from work?

## Personal Touch

Taking short, frequent breaks throughout the day is one of the best and simplest methods for managing your own stress.

# KEEPING THE FIRES BURNING

## In a Nutshell

Participants learn how to fight job burnout by envisioning and planning small changes in their workplace or job definition.

## Time

20-30 minutes.

## What You'll Need

You may want to make overheads of pages 82 and 83.

## What to Do

Explain to the participants that burnout is one of the most serious problems that we face in the organizational environment, and it's main cause is stress. Then proceed to explain that the key to fighting this stress is the Small-Change Principle, which is, like all good principles, quite simple: *Small changes can have BIG outcomes* (page 82).

Show the overhead on page 83 to illustrate the Small-

Change Principle. Seen right-side up, it looks side a happy face, but upside-down, it looks like a sad face.

Now present the following case to the group.

> *Maryann had been an administrative assistant for five years, but gradually she had grown to hate her job. She felt that she was consistently treated unfairly, blamed for things that weren't her fault, and put under more pressure than she could bear. A consultant discovered that Maryann made an average of ten trips to the photocopy room each day, where she often encountered long lines or broken machines. Her boss was not very sympathetic, even though she told him about copy problems many times. The entire image she had of her job seemed to revolve around problems related to the copy machines. Rather than lose her, her boss agreed to provide a small copier for Maryann's workstation. She felt vindicated, and, more important, the pattern of her workday changed dramatically for the better.*

In your discussion, point out how small, isolated factors lead to very broad, overly general impressions of the workplace experience.

Following the discussion, have participants create a list of small changes they would like to see in their workplace that might make a big difference in their workplace experience. Have people share some of the their suggestions, and explore the feasibility of implementing them.

## Discussion Questions

1. What is burnout?
2. What is the Small-Change Principle? What are some examples?
3. How could the Small-Change Principle be used to protect you from burnout?
4. What are other ways to protect yourself from burnout?

## If You're Short on Time

To make this a 10-minute exercise, (a) shorten the introduction, (b) have people make a list of small changes, and (c) call on a few people to share portions of their list with the group.

## Tip!

Remember:

*For want of a nail, the shoe was lost.*
*For want of a shoe, the horse was lost.*
*For want of the horse, the rider was lost.*
*For want of the rider, the message was lost.*
*For want of the message, the battle was lost.*
*For want of the battle, the war was lost.*

# THE SMALL CHANGE PRINCIPLE

"Small changes can produce **BIG** outcomes."

# THE LAUGH GRAPH

## In a Nutshell

Participants imagine themselves at work and rate their stress levels. Then, after some stand-up comedy—starring both the leader and some participants—they rate their stress levels again.

## Time

About 20 minutes, depending on just how much fun you want to have.

## What You'll Need

A good supply of jokes is all you'll need. If you like, you can depend on the members of your group for this material. They might be more likely to laugh at their own jokes, anyway.

## What to Do

Ask participants to imagine themselves in a stressful work situation and have them rate their stress level on a scale of 1 to 5, where 5 is the highest level of stress.

Next, remind participants that humor lowers stress, boosts our immune systems, has no negative side effects, and feels good, too.

Then start the serious stand-up routine. If you like, you can make it an "open mike" night, with participation from your group members. About 10 minutes of jokes is all you'll need, but you can continue as long as you've got good material.

Then ask participants to rate their stress level once again. Compute a quick average, and plot it on your display graph. Has the average stress level dropped?

Here is a sample joke you may want to include in your material:

*Interview Joke*

*Reaching the end of the job interview, the Human Resources person asked the young MBA, "And what starting salary were you looking for?"*

*The candidate responded confidently, "In the neighborhood of $150,000 a year, depending on the benefits package."*

*The interviewer said, "Well, what would you say to a benefits package of five weeks vacation, fourteen paid holidays, full medical and dental, company matching retirement fund to 50 percent of salary, and a company car leased every two years—say a red Corvette to start?"*

*The graduate sat up, mouth agape, and said, "Wow! Are you kidding?"*

*And the interviewer responded, "Of course ... but you started it!"*

## Discussion Questions

1. How might humor help you in the workplace?
2. How has humor defused difficult situations in your personal life or work situation?
3. How can you add more laughter to your life?

## If You Have More Time

Here is some other material you might want to use.

*Salesman Joke*

*A traveling salesman rings the doorbell and 10-year-old Johnny answers, holding a beer and smoking a fat cigar. The salesman says, "Little boy, is your mother home?"*

*Little Johnny taps his ash on the carpet and says, "What do you think?"*

## A Selection of Dilbert's Laws

*"A pat on the back is only a few centimeters from a kick in the butt."*

*"Don't be irreplaceable, if you can't be replaced, you can't be promoted."*

*"Eat one live toad the first thing in the morning and nothing worse will happen to you the rest of the day."*

*"If at first you don't succeed, try again. Then quit. No use being a damn fool about it."*

*"Never delay the ending of a meeting or the beginning of a cocktail hour."*

*"If you are good, you will be assigned all the work. If you are really good, you will get out of it."*

*"If it wasn't for the last minute, nothing would get done."*

**Tip!**

The Internet is an unlimited source of fresh funny material.

# A LITTLE HELP
# FROM MY FRIENDS

## In a Nutshell

Participants are asked to write an "MST Plan," which outlines how colleagues in the workplace might work together to help each other cope with and reduce stress.

## Time

20 minutes.

## What You'll Need

Writing materials for each participant.

## What to Do

Explain that no one feels more alone than the person under stress. Then proceed to introduce the concept of the MST, or Mutual Support Team.

An MST is an informal team created to provide mutual support among its members. It works positively and constructively to increase the stress-management skills of its members, to reduce sources of stress, and to provide mutual support in time of stress.

Ask members to complete MST Plans—plans for assembling Mutual Support Teams in their particular work environments. The plan should suggest some possible members (by name), possible meeting times (during or after work hours, depending on the situation), and specific activities, functions, and goals of the team.

Ask a few people to share their plans with the group, and lead a brief discussion about the feasibility and possible benefits of the plans.

## If You Have More Time

You can expand the exercise by organizing real or simulated Mutual Support Teams. Have the teams meet and work up detailed plans for activities, roles, functions, and goals.

## Discussion Questions

1. What roles, activities, functions, and goals do you foresee for your Mutual Support Team?
2. How frequently do you believe an MST should meet, and in what setting?
3. How might an MST have helped you in the past? How might it protect you from stress in the future?

## Tip!

Remember, an MST is not a gripe group!

# THE MAKE-A-FIST TECHNIQUE

## In a Nutshell

Participants learn a quick, simply muscle relaxation method that people can use at their desks.

## Time

10 minutes.

## What You'll Need

No special materials are needed.

## What to Do

Explain that one of the simplest ways to achieve a relaxed state is to relax one's muscles. One way to relax muscles is to *stretch* them, and another way is to *tense and release* them.

When you tense a muscle group vigorously for a few seconds and then *release* the tension in that muscle group, the muscles, now exhausted, will be in a more relaxed state than they were before you tensed them.

With participants seated in a relaxed posture, have them tighten the left fist, hold the tension for a slow count of five, then *slowly release* the tension.

Then have them do the same with the right fist. Continue in this fashion, moving through the body: to the arms, the face, the tummy, the buttocks, the legs, and the feet.

Ask a few people where they usually carry their tension, and do the exercise again for those body parts. Lead a brief discussion about the outcome, advantages, and possible applications of this technique.

## Discussion Questions

1. Is it possible to feel tense, even though one's muscles are relaxed?
2. How do we benefit by relaxing our muscles?
3. How does the Make-a-Fist Technique make you feel?

## Personal Touch

This is an ideal technique to try on your own. Just clench and relax. Where can you use this technique? How might it help?

# MAKE ME LAUGH

## In a Nutshell

Participants work in teams to explore ways in which humor can be used to improve unpleasant situations.

## Time

20-30 minutes.

## What You'll Need

Writing materials for participants.

## What to Do

Remind participants how humor can be used to reinterpret what's happening or to defuse a tense situation.

Now, divide the group into teams.

Have each team (a) write down three stressful situations of their own choosing (for example, interpersonal conflict, some problem with a boss, the failure of a project, or a tight deadline), and (b) explore ways in which humor might be used to improve the situation.

Call on a representative from some or all of the groups to report to the entire group, and lead a discussion about the outcomes.

## Discussion Questions

1. Has humor ever gotten you out of a tight spot? What happened?
2. How might humor help in a tough situation? How might it hurt?

## Alternative

You might want to have each team pick one scenario to role play. You can then have a few teams present their role plays to the entire group.

## If You're Short on Time

Give two or three examples of stressful situations, and ask for suggestions for using humor to improve those situations.

# MAKING IT PERSONAL

## In a Nutshell

Participants learn how to design a daily personal relaxation routine.

## Time

15-20 minutes.

## What You'll Need

Distribute a typical daily calendar page or a copy of page 97.

## What to Do

Remind participants that the best techniques are *proactive*—that is, they protect you from stress before you're even exposed to it. That's why it's important to get into a regular routine of stress-management, rather than waiting for something to go wrong.

Next, have participants complete the calendar page, listing stress-management and relaxation techniques they can perform on a regular schedule.

Provide some guidelines by asking various questions: What kinds of techniques could you see yourself performing first thing in the morning? For a few seconds here and there during the early part of the day? During an extended break time? Over lunch? Late in the day? Before and after meetings? When you get home? Before bed?

Call on a few people to present their strategies, and discuss these with the group.

You may want to display a list of techniques on a screen to remind people of the range of techniques they have available.

## Discussion Questions

1. What kinds of techniques could you do at home?
2. How many minutes a day do you think you should spend managing stress?
3. Other than calendars, what methods might you use to make sure you practice stress-management and relaxation techniques every day?

## If You're Short on Time

Display a calendar on a screen, and ask for suggestions for scheduling brief stress-management and relaxation exercises. Distribute copies of page 97 for people to fill out on their own.

## *Personal Stress-Management Regimen*
### Exercise: "Making It Personal"

| Time | STRESS-MANAGEMENT ACTIVITY |
|---|---|
| "B.W."<br>(*Before Work*) | |
| ———— | |
| ———— | |
| ———— | |
| ———— | |
| ———— | |
| "A.W."<br>(*After Work*) | |

# MEDITATION FOR THE IMPATIENT

## In a Nutshell

Participants learn Benson's relaxation technique, focusing on breathing while silently saying the word "one" with each exhalation.

## Time

10 minutes.

## What You'll Need

No special materials are required.

## What to Do

Explain that meditation does not have to be a complicated ordeal to be effective. Some of the emotional and physiological benefits of meditation can be obtained simply by (a) sitting in a relaxed position with your eyes closed, (b) breathing in and out slowly through your nose, (c) focusing your attention on your breathing, and (d) silently saying the word "one" each time you exhale. This is the method pioneered by

Harvard medical researcher Herbert Benson.

Have your participants practice this technique for 5 minutes.

Afterwards, call on a few people to evaluate their reactions to the technique, and lead a brief discussion about the possible uses of the technique during the work day.

## Discussion Questions

1.  How does Benson's technique make you feel? Does it relax you?
2.  How can you incorporate this simple form of meditation into your work day?

## Alternative

To demonstrate the power of the technique, break up the five minutes into one-minute intervals. Before they start to meditate, have them put a check mark on a relaxation scale, indicating their current level of tension. Signal the group quietly at the end of each minute, and ask participants to open their eyes briefly and place a check mark on their relaxation scales indicating their current level of tension. At the end of 5 minutes, call on a few people to see what the average score was at the beginning and at the end of the exercise. You should find, on the average, a gradual decrease in tension level.

## Personal Touch

Don't forget to try Benson's relaxation technique on your own. If you're intrigued by meditation, sign up for a course at your local adult education program.

# THE NIRVANA ROOM

## In a Nutshell

Participants identify ways of making their work environments less stressful.

## Time

15 minutes.

## What You'll Need

Participants will need writing materials.

## What to Do

Remind participants that the best work spaces can create a sense of calm, while keeping productivity high. Now, present the following five principles (see the overhead on page 106):

1. *The Irritation Principle:* Stimuli that irritate the senses can cause stress. Examples: loud noises, echoes, clashing colors.

2. *The Soothing Principle:* Stimuli that soothe the senses can relieve stress. Examples: soft music, dim lighting, silky textures, garden scents.

3. *The Overstimulation Principle:* Overstimulation can cause stress. Examples: several people speaking simultaneously, the sound of many machines operating.

4. *The Minimal Principle:* Low stimulation can relieve stress. Examples: being alone in a quiet room, being alone on the shore of a lake.

5. *The Colorful Principle:* A soothing color scheme can relieve stress. Examples: low-saturation colors, "cool" colors (in the blue-green range), and Baker-Miller pink.

Have people write down at least one stress-reducing change that could be made in their current work environment. Ask a few people to share their ideas.

## Discussion Questions

1. Are there certain colors, textures, or patterns that make you feel stressed? That make you feel relaxed?
2. What sounds make you feel stressed? What sounds relax you?
3. What changes, large and small, can be made in your work environment to make you feel more relaxed?

# Tip!

Keep individual differences in mind; what's irritating to one person might be soothing to another.

# Environmental stress principles

- **THE** IRRITATION **PRINCIPLE**

- **THE** *soothing* **PRINCIPLE**

- **THE OVERSTIMULATION** PRINCIPLE

- **THE** MINIMAL **PRINCIPLE**

- **THE COLORFUL PRINCIPLE**

# ONE MINUTE IN HELL

## In a Nutshell

Participants learn how powerful a relaxation technique can be in helping us get through uncomfortable situations. Participants grasp an ice cube in one hand for one minute. After a short break, they repeat this while doing a relaxation exercise.

## Time

5-10 minutes.

## What You'll Need

You'll need one ice cube for every one in the audience, along with buckets to distribute the ice and collect the remnants. You'll also need a stopwatch.

## What to Do

Distribute ice cubes to every participant. As soon as everyone has a cube, ask people to grasp it tightly in one hand, and encourage them to keep holding.

After a minute has passed, tell them they can let go. Ask two or three people to tell you how it felt to hold the ice cube.

Now repeat the exercise, this time talking people through a simple breathing or imagery exercise. Be sure to have participants switch hands for the second round.

One simple way to proceed is to have people focus on their breathing. When a minute has elapsed, have people release the ice cubes. While the remnants are being collected, ask people how the second experience compared to the first.

## Discussion Questions

1. Why does a breathing technique (or another relaxation exercise) make it easier to bear discomfort?
2. How are relaxation methods used to aid modern childbirth?
3. How might you use a relaxation technique to help you weather difficult situations in your life?

## Personal Touch

If you're on your own, you can still try this procedure just as it's described.

# THE PLACE OF PERFECT PEACE

## In a Nutshell

Participants are asked to envision a private "place of peace," real or imaginary, and then to focus on and examine that image to help them relax.

## Time

10 minutes.

## What You'll Need

No special materials are needed.

## What to Do

Have participants sit in a relaxed position, close their eyes, and breathe easily. Then begin in a soothing voice:

*Relax, breathe easily, and clear your minds. I'm now going to take you to a special place, a place where you are safe.... It's a place of perfect peace... a place where you have no cares... a place where your body and your mind are perfectly*

*relaxed.... Continue to relax and breathe easily....
Now continue on your journey to that special place,
that place of perfect peace.... You're there now,
safe and serene in this special place, this perfect
place, this peaceful place, this place of perfect
peace.... Look around you slowly.... What do you
see to your left... in front of you... to your right...?
What kinds of sounds do you hear...? What
textures do you feel against your skin...? What
odors do you smell...? Look around you slowly,
and continue to relax. Feel the relaxation surround
you in this special place, this place of perfect
peace.... Continue to relax, and feel the magic of
this special place....*

After a pause of a minute or so, gradually bring your
participants back to the present environment. Lead a
brief discussion about people's experiences, but don't
ask them to reveal the location of their special place.
Did everyone find this place? How did it make them
feel? Could they conjure up this image on their own on
breaks at work?

## Discussion Questions

1.  How did the exercise make you feel? Did it relax
    you?
2.  Could you call up this image in the future? Will you
    need a tape, or could you do it on your own?
3.  When might you call up this image to help you fight
    stress? What effect might the exercise have?

# Personal Touch

If you like, put this text on tape, and play it when you'd like to escape to that place of perfect peace.

# POPEYE PUFFS

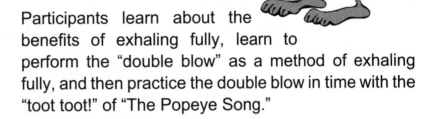

## In a Nutshell

Participants learn about the benefits of exhaling fully, learn to perform the "double blow" as a method of exhaling fully, and then practice the double blow in time with the "toot toot!" of "The Popeye Song."

## Time

5-10 minutes.

## What You'll Need

No special materials are required.

## What to Do

First, explain the rationale: When times get tough, our first response is to breathe shallowly, which means that we rebreathe excessively. Deliberately controlling one's breathing is a powerful way to keep control of one's mood, and the simplest way to assure the right mix of gases in your blood to make sure that you occasionally *exhale fully*.

Next, explain and demonstrate the "double blow." When you forcibly blow out all of the air in your lungs, there's still some air left. In the double blow, we blow out all the air, then, before we inhale, we blow hard once more. The torso is somewhat curled at this point, with the air apparently coming from the abdominal area. The point is to reset the respiratory system so that you stop rebreathing old air. Have people try this.

Finally—and have some fun with this—have the group sing "The Popeye Song," doing the double blow when Popeye normally does his "toot toot." Sing it a few times, with clapping, hand gestures, and body movement. Here is the basic verse:

*I'm Popeye the sailor man, (puff puff)*
*I'm Popeye the sailor man, (puff puff)*
*I'm strong to the finish,*
*'cause I eats me spinach,*
*I'm Popeye the sailor man! (puff puff)*

## Discussion Questions

1. What are the dangers of rebreathing? Of shallow breathing? Of hyperventilating?
2. Why is a double blow better than a single blow?
3. In what situations are you more likely to breathe improperly? How could you use the double blow as a quick corrective?
4. How long does it take to do a double blow? When might you use it during the day?

# PUNCH THAT PILLOW!

## In a Nutshell

Participants punch pillows, squeeze flour-filled balloons, throw foam balls, shoot rubber bands, and so on, while they imagine letting go of hostile or negative feelings.

## Time

10 minutes.

## What You'll Need

An assortment of objects that can safely be punched, thrown, stretched, squeezed, or otherwise abused. Small foam pillows work well.

## What to Do

Explain to participants that one way to get the body back into a relaxed state is to do some relaxation exercises, but another may be to *act out the hostility in a non-destructive way*.

Now have participants pound, pull, stretch, batter, and

throw. They can also make sound effects like *Pow!* and *Wham!* This should all be done in fun.

The purpose is to give people some experience with materials they can use for non-destructive expression of negative feelings. For most of the people, this will be the first time they've done something like this since they were young children.

Ask a few participants to describe physical outlets that they currently use to relieve stress. Then discuss which activities they might be able to engage in on a regular basis to help them relieve stress.

## Discussion Questions

1. Why is it unnecessary to imagine a victim when you punch a pillow?
2. What bodily state are you relieving by punching a pillow?
3. How might you use regular athletic activity to redirect negative feelings?

## Tip!

While participants are "playing," emphasize that they need *not* imagine a victim for the exercise to be valuable. They're simply *releasing tension* in the body. They can do this *without* imagining that they're choking their boss.

## Personal Touch

Even without a group, you can practice pillow punching and other non-destructive methods of expressing hostility.

# REACH FOR THE SKY

## In a Nutshell

Participants learn to use active stretching to relieve muscle tension.

## Time

5-10 minutes.

## What You'll Need

No special materials or supplies are required.

## What to Do

You might find it helpful to begin this exercise by reviewing the difference between passive and active stretches: Briefly, passive stretches rely on gravity and breathing techniques to produce slow, relaxing stretches (see "Gravity Magic," page 67). In an active stretch—which is the more common type of stretch—we tense muscles in order to pull or push part of the body into a stretched position.

Demonstrate some active stretches, and then lead the group in performing these stretches.

Reach both arms high, then stretch the entire left side of the body, through the leg, torso, arm, and fingers, as far as possible toward the ceiling, inhaling as you stretch.

Hold this position for a count of three, relax and exhale for a count of three, and then repeat the stretch with the right side of the body.

After you've shifted from left to right three times, repeat the stretch with both sides at once, holding for a count of five. Then, easily and gradually, bend forward and lower your arms to the ground (no need to try to touch the toes).

Generally, you can augment each stretch by inhaling during the stretch, and augment relaxation by exhaling as you release each stretch.

Be sure to caution participants not to apply too much force to the stretches, especially if they're out of shape or have poor flexibility.

They can gradually increase the length of the stretch over a period of weeks, if they wish. Also emphasize how important it is to release a stretch slowly and gradually. Forcing a stretch can damage muscles, ligaments, or tendons, and so can releasing a stretch too abruptly.

# Discussion Questions

1. Why do passive stretches often produce more of a relaxation effect than active stretches?
2. Which stretches involve more risk—active or passive?
3. Do you currently perform active stretches as part of your daily routine? How might you incorporate these stretches into your routine?

# Tip!

Above all, make sure participants don't bounce. Bouncing is the quickest way to do damage.

# Personal Touch

Active stretches can be used throughout the day. Practice a few on your own and try to fit them in your schedule.

# READY, SET, SIT!

## In a Nutshell

Participants learn that sitting in certain positions at their desks can be profoundly relaxing, while other positions can aggravate stress. They are encouraged to assume a special "relaxation posture" for a few minutes each day to help immunize them against stress.

## Time

20 minutes.

## What You'll Need

Participants should be seated during this exercise, and two chairs should be set up in the front of the room, facing the group. You may want to use a blackboard or flipchart to enhance the presentation. It would be helpful to have a clock or timer handy that has a second hand or a digital readout in seconds.

## What to Do

Invite a member of the group to come forward to sit in

one of the two chairs in the front of the room, and assume a very uncomfortable and unnatural sitting position. Sit in the other chair, assume the same position, and direct everyone in the group to do the same. The position should be held for about a full minute, if possible, after which the group should be asked to rate how tense they feel on a scale of 1 (very relaxed) to 10 (very tense).

Repeat this procedure with other volunteers and other uncomfortable, awkward positions, as time allows. Some of the positions may be comical, so have fun with them.

Get a quick tally of the scores and list them on a blackboard or flipchart. Now explain that in recent years researchers have discovered some ideal positions—called "relaxation postures"—that make people feel incredibly relaxed. These positions even produce some of the same physiological changes that meditation produces.

Demonstrate such a posture, and direct the group to follow: First, bring your heels together on the floor in front of you, and then let your feet separate naturally, so they're at about a ninety-degree angle with respect to each other. Next, face your palms toward the ceiling, let your fingers curl up naturally, and gently drop your hands onto your lap. Let your shoulders relax, but there's no need to slump forward. Let your jaw go slack, so that your mouth is open a bit. Finally, just close your eyes. Breathe normally.

After a minute or so, have people open their eyes and ask them how they feel. Lead a discussion about how the relaxation posture might be used throughout the day to immunize people against stress.

## Discussion Questions

1. Which comes first, stress or an awkward sitting posture?
2. Can an awkward sitting position cause stress?
3. How might you use the relaxation posture to help you relax during the day?

## Personal Touch

Teach yourself this simple "relaxation posture," and practice it frequently. Try comparing this posture to some awkward ones, just as the exercise suggests.

# RED, WHITE, AND VERY BLUE

## In a Nutshell

Participants sort color tiles in order from least stressful to most stressful.

## Time

5-10 minutes.

## What You'll Need

Each participant will need an envelope containing small (about 2 inches square) color "tiles," which can easily be made with a paper cutter. Each set of tiles should be identical and should contain eight tiles: black, white, and six basic rainbow colors (violet, blue, green, red, orange, and yellow). They can be stored and distributed in small envelopes.

## What to Do

Remind participants that we tend not to think about color very much when we think about sources of stress, but studies show that the colors that surround us—the colors of the walls, the colors of the furniture, even the colors of the papers that we write on—have a definite impact on our mood.

Distribute the color packets, and ask people to sort the colors in order from what seem to be the *least stressful* to the *most stressful*. Ask for a show of hands to see how many people have the blue on top (many hands should go up). Ask to see how many people have the yellow on top (fewer hands should go up).

Now ask people to re-sort the colors in order from what seem to be the *most energizing* versus the *least energizing*. Find out what color turns up on top most frequently (probably red). Find out what color turns up on the bottom most frequently (probably blue or violet).

Continue by leading a discussion about how to design or modify a work environment that uses color to *energize us* when we need to be energized and to *relax us* when we need to be relaxed.

## Discussion Questions

1. What kind of color scheme might energize you when you need to be energized and relax you when you need to relax?
2. How can we accommodate people whose color preferences don't fit the norm?
3. What are some advantages and disadvantages of decorating the workplace exclusively in soothing colors? Exclusively in energizing colors?
4. How does the design of your current workplace

affect your mood?  How might it be improved?

## If You Have More Time

Divide the group into teams of four or five people, and give the teams 15 minutes to plan ideal color schemes for their work environment.  Have a representative of some or all of the teams report his or her  team's recommendations to the entire group.

## Alternative

Bring a lamp and some colored bulbs with you to the training room.  Extinguish the room lights and illuminate the room in blue, red, or other colors.  Ask people for their reactions to various colors.

## Tip!

Remember, color's effect on performance is minimal. People type just about as fast in a blue room as in a red room.  But they'll probably *feel better* in the former.

## Personal Touch

Make the color tiles, and order them from least to most stressful.  Then decorate your home and work spaces to achieve the calm—or the energy!—you desire.

# RUN FOR YOUR LIFE!

## In a Nutshell

Participants learn some simple exercises and compose plans for performing them, and teams suggest ways the organization might offer resources to facilitate employee exercise.

## Time

10 minutes.

## What You'll Need

No special materials are needed.

## What to Do

Get a show of hands to see how many people feel a little stressed. Have people walk or run in place (depending on their ability) for 3 minutes.

Now have them *wait* 30 seconds or so, and ask again for the show of hands. Fewer people should now report feeling stressed.

Explain the benefits of getting some exercise during the work day. Remind participants that vigorous physical activity can serve as a proactive means of fighting stress by improving overall health and well-being, and it can serve as a reactive means of fighting stress by serving as a constructive outlet for aggressive tendencies.

## Discussion Questions

1. What effect does vigorous exercise have on your mood?
2. Do you currently get any vigorous exercise during the work day, either at work or elsewhere? What kind and how much?
3. How might you incorporate vigorous exercise into your work day?

## If You Have More Time

Divide the group up into teams of between three and five members, and have the teams spend a few minutes working out ways that their organization might encourage employee exercise: for example, by placing exercise bicycles or stepping machines in common areas. Have a representative from each team report the team's ideas to the group.

Here is a list of simple, non-taxing exercises that can be performed in an office environment. Add other examples as you learn about them, especially if they're suggested by members of your group.

*Exercises*

*Knee lifts, performed standing in place*
*Jogging in place*
*Jumping jacks*
*Stepping (requires a step platform)*
*Bicycling (requires a stationary bicycle)*
*Rowing (requires a rowing machine)*
*Squats*

## Personal Touch

Learn and practice your own movement routines to help manage stress at work and at home.

# THE SEEK AND KILL GAME

## In a Nutshell

Participants learn how to identify and eliminate sources of stress in their professional and personal lives.

## Time

15 minutes.

## What You'll Need

Writing materials for all participants.

## What to Do

Explain that much of the stress we feel comes from the "stressors" that surround us. Stressors are environmental events—like criticisms, cigarette smoke, loud noises, muggers, and bills—that threaten us in some way.

The relationship between stress and stressors is only approximate. At times we experience stress in the absence of any obvious stressors, and we might not feel any stress at all when confronted by real threats.

Generally, though, where there's stress there are stressors.

Tell participants that there's a special approach to managing stress, and that is to get rid of the stressors. When you're being chased by a lion, you could do a breathing exercise to keep yourself somewhat calm, but you could also shoot the lion. No lion, no stress.

Ask participants for examples of stressors, taking care to help them distinguish between *stress*, which is an internal state, and *stressors*, which are external events and objects.

Then ask participants to list perceived threats in the left-hand column on their paper and constructive ways to eliminate or curtail these apparent threats in the right-hand column. Give people between 5 and 10 minutes to make their lists. Then ask volunteers to present a few items from their lists. Ask the group to react to the volunteers' plans for eliminating stressors.

## Discussion Questions

1.  How are stress and stressors related to each other? Can you feel stress even though you're not exposed to any real threats? Can you be exposed to stressors without experiencing a stress reaction?
2.  Can all stressors in your environment be eliminated or curtailed? Which ones can? Which ones can't?
3.  How would you curtail or eliminate stressors in your environment?

## Personal Touch

Even without a group, you can—and should!—complete this exercise. List your own sources of stress, and try to devise ways of minimizing or eliminating them.

# STACKED TO THE CEILING

## In a Nutshell

Working in small groups, participants help each other solve problems of disorganization.

## Time

20 minutes.

## What You'll Need

Copies of the handout on page 141 for every participant.

## What to Do

Remind participants that *disorganization* is one of the major sources of stress in our lives. Anything you can do—even something very small—to get yourself better organized will likely reduce the stress you're feeling.

Distribute handout on page 141 to the participants. Have a volunteer describe a problem of disorganization, and ask the group for fixes.

List these items on a display board, and from these

suggestions create a *second* list that contains some general organizing principles. As time permits, repeat this process with other volunteers.

## Discussion Questions

1. How can disorganization lead to stress?
2. What's your favorite organizing trick or tool?
3. What's your worst organizing problem? How might you solve it?

## Tip!

Remember, *"People who keep lists of things to do, do more things."*

## Personal Touch

Disorganized? Take yourself through the exercise by listing areas where you need improvement and seeking ways to change.

# GETTING ORGANIZED

- CALENDARS, SCHEDULING SOFTWARE, PDAs
- LISTS OF THINGS TO DO
- LABEL TASKS WITH PRIORITY STATUS
- SEEK REMINDERS FROM COLLEAGUES
- POST NOTES, AFFIRMATIONS

- SEND YOURSELF NOTES, AFFIRMATIONS
- LEAVE MESSAGES ON YOUR VOICE MAIL
- CREATE ADEQUATE SHELF AND FILE SPACE
- KEEP FREQUENTLY USED ITEMS CLOSE BY
- KEEP IMPORTANT ITEMS IN SPECIAL PLACES

- SCHEDULE DAILY TIME FOR PLANNING
- ALWAYS CARRY A RECORDING DEVICE
- ALWAYS CARRY BACKUP BATTERIES
- MAKE DAILY, WEEKLY, MONTHLY, YEARLY PLANS

- DIVIDE UP DIFFICULT TASKS INTO SMALL ONES
- SCHEDULE EXERCISE TIME
- SCHEDULE RELAXATION TIME
- WHAT WORKS FOR YOU?

# STAYING COOL, GETTING HOT

## In a Nutshell

Participants learn about simple, inexpensive temperature monitors for tracking and controlling stress.

## Time

5-10 minutes.

## What You'll Need

You'll need at least one temperature monitor per participant to conduct this exercise. The good news is that you can obtain minimally suitable devices for as little as 25 cents each. Here are some suggestions for devices and vendors.

### *Devices*

Stress-Control Biofeedback Card® ($1.00 to $3.00 each, depending on quantity purchased)

StressDots® Card ($2.00 to $3.00 each)

Stress Therapy™ Card (about $2.00 each)

Biotic-Band® II (about $5.00 each)

Hand-Held Alcohol Thermometers (25 to 40 cents each)

Mood Rings ($3.00 to $4.00 each)

*Vendors*

The Stens Corporation
www.stens-biofeedback.com
1-800-25-STENS

Bio-Medical Instruments
www.biofeedback-bmi.com
1-800-521-4640

SRS Medical Systems
www.srsmedical.com
1-800-345-5642

## What to Do

Explain that when we're stressed, our muscles are tense and taught, and blood doesn't flow very easily to our extremities.  Thus, the skin temperature of our fingers is very sensitive to the arousal state of our body.  When we're relaxed, blood flows easily to the extremities, which *raises* the skin temperature.  When we're tense, blood has trouble reaching the extremities, which *lowers* the skin temperature.

Distribute the dots, cards, rings, or bands of your choice. Have people squeeze the device until they've got a stable color, and then talk them through abdominal breathing or an imagery exercise. Ask people who were able to shift to a more relaxed color to raise their hands.

## Discussion Questions

1. Why does skin temperature in the extremities (like the tips of the fingers) increase when we're relaxed?
2. How can biofeedback devices help us achieve deeper states of relaxation?
3. How might you use a temperature-sensitive biofeedback device (such as a thermometer, card, band, dot, or ring) to help you relax during the day?

## If You're Short on Time

Skip the relaxation exercise and have people trade temperature monitors with people who've produced colors different from theirs. Have them hold the new monitor (their own color should reappear), and then trade back.

## Tip!

For up-to-date information, try searching the Internet using the keywords "biofeedback devices." Ideally, you'll let the members of your group keep these devices, but if your budget is tight, you can always collect them at the conclusion of the exercise.

## Personal Touch

You won't get the bulk rate, but you can buy just one temperature sensor and use it as a biofeedback device to help you manage your own stress.

# TANGERINE TREES

## In a Nutshell

Participants relax while you talk them through a colorful journey through a fanciful world, after which you lead a discussion about how this technique might be used in the workplace.

## Time

10 minutes.

## What You'll Need

No special materials or supplies are required.

## What to Do

Have people get into a relaxed position. You may want to use a "relaxation posture" (see "Ready, Set, Sit!" page 123). Finally, ask participants to close their eyes, and recite the following text in a soothing voice:

*Relax, breathe easily, and clear your minds.... I'm going to take you on a journey to a strange and beautiful place, a place where you'll feel peaceful and calm, free of all worry.... Breathe slowly and easily, and let your bodies relax.... That's good.... Now here we go....*

*All around you, there is nothing... just darkness... a soothing blackness... a peaceful silence.... Look around you and absorb the blackness... and listen to the silence, while you continue to breathe easily.... Gradually, very gradually, you begin to see a hint of color among the blackness, as if a very dim light has been lit far away.... The color is reddish-orange, very dim and very beautiful. It's all around you, a soft, dim, reddish-orange glow.... Look around you slowly and absorb this beautiful glow.... As the glow begins to get brighter, you begin to hear a gentle sshhhhh sound in the air around you... the whispery sound of a light breeze, of gently moving air.... Absorb this gentle, peaceful sssshhhh, while you continue to admire the beautiful reddish-orange glow....*

*Gradually, very gradually, the dim glow is starting to get a little brighter, as if the sun is just beginning to peek above a distant horizon. But you don't see any sun, just this beautiful glow... reddish-orange all around you.... Focus on the glow, and listen to the gentle sssshhhh in the air around you. Now, with the glow getting brighter, you can just begin to make out the outlines of objects in the distance. Slowly and gradually, the objects become clearer.... Embedded in the beautiful reddish-orange glow are the outlines of extraordinary trees,*

*trees like none you've ever seen before.... As the glow gradually gets brighter, you can begin to make out the details of the trees. There are thousands of trees, off in the distance... beautiful, elegant trees of great size.... The trees, illuminated by the glowing light, are all intensely orange in color.... Each tree has hundreds of limbs and branches, long and old and gnarled and intertwined, like long slender arms embracing each other in a hundred ways.... The branches are all different shades of orange, tinged with red, and dotted with small clusters of star-shaped leaves... all glowing softly in the gentle reddish-orange light. The gentle ssshhhh sound, you now realize, is made by the air jostling the clusters of star-shaped leaves.*

*Looking at the gnarled, glowing branches makes you feel a great peace.... Listen to the gentle ssshhhh of the rustling star-shaped leaves, and feel the peace of the curved and gnarled branches and limbs of the great trees.... Absorb the calm of the reddish-orange glow that surrounds the beautiful trees and fills the space around your body... that gradually, very gradually, begins to fill your body with a soothing, gentle, glowing feeling of peace. Feel the reddish-orange peace, and relax....*

*Hold the peace inside you, as you slowly, very slowly, open your eyes....*

## Discussion Questions

1. How might you be able to use audio tapes to help you use guided imagery?
2. How might you use this image to help you manage stress during the workday?
3. What other images might you use to help you relax?

## Alternative

You may want to put your image text on audio tape. In your session, you can play the tape instead of reciting the text.

## Personal Touch

You can also use the tape for yourself! Get selfish!

# THE TEN-YEAR PLANNER

## In a Nutshell

Participants complete a ten-year personal and professional plan, in order to help them make decisions and keep perspective on daily affairs.

## Time

20 minutes.

## What You'll Need

Copies of the handout on page 154, along with scrap paper, should be distributed to all participants.

## What to Do

Distribute scrap paper and copies of the handout, and have participants spend about 10 minutes completing the form, briefly listing specific plans for both their professional and personal lives for the next ten years. Assure participants that they'll be able to keep the forms; you *won't* be collecting them.

When they're done, ask a few volunteers to share

some items from their plans. Ask your group members to share any surprises they may have experienced when completing the form.

Next, ask for suggestions about how these plans might be used to help reduce or cope with stress. List the suggestions on a display board. To complete the discussion, you might want to display your own list on an overhead. Here's a partial list.

1) Attach it to your personal calendar to help keep you on track.
2) Use it to help you make daily decisions.
3) Use it to help you keep minor problems in perspective.

## Discussion Questions

1. How far ahead do you normally plan your life? Do you do this in writing?
2. What are some entries on your ten-year plan that you're willing to share?
3. Were you surprised at any point by what you wrote on this plan? How so?
4. How might you use this plan to help you eliminate sources of stress in your life?

## Alternative

Depending on the group and the context, you might want to adjust the time period on the planner. Five years might be enough to prove your point. If your participants are very young, you might to use a 20-year planner.

## Personal Touch

Don't forget to make your own Ten-Year Plan. It's a great way to get perspective on daily affairs.

# Ten-Year Plan

Starting Date:_____

| Year | Personal Plan | Professional Plan |
|------|---------------|-------------------|
| 1 | | |
| 2 | | |
| 3 | | |
| 4 | | |
| 5 | | |
| 6 | | |
| 7 | | |
| 8 | | |
| 9 | | |
| 10 | | |

# TERRIFIC TUMMY TECHNIQUE

## In a Nutshell

Participants learn a powerful relaxation technique called abdominal breathing.

## Time

10-15 minutes.

## What You'll Need

No special materials or supplies are required.

## What to Do

Tell the participants that they are going to learn a new way to breathe, sometimes called *abdominal* or *diaphragmatic* breathing: inhaling and exhaling by expanding and contracting the abdominal area, while keeping the chest still. Breathing in this way has some remarkable, almost magical, relaxation benefits.

For reasons that are not clearly understood, holding the chest still while forcing the abdominal area to expand and contract as you breathe has significant and

**155**

speedy relaxation benefits. Breathing abdominally for just two or three minutes raises the skin temperature in your fingertips (by relaxing blood vessels and improving circulation), lowers pulse rate, and makes you feel more relaxed.

With one hand on your chest and the other on your abdomen, show the group how to breathe by keeping the upper hand motionless. Exaggerate the expansion and contraction of the abdominal area as you inhale and exhale. Then ask your participants to do the same. Praise people for complying, and point out good examples to the group. Provide coaching as necessary to help people comply.

## Discussion Questions

1. Why is breathing with the chest often a sign of stress?
2. What steps might you take to make abdominal breathing a part of your daily routine?
3. Why do you think abdominal breathing tends to reduce stress?

## Personal Touch

Put one hand on your abdomen, the other on your chest, and start breathing. (See above!) This is one of the simplest and most powerful personal stress-management techniques around.

# THIS PERFECT DAY

## In a Nutshell

Participants visualize a "perfect," stress-free day, from morning until night.

## Time

5-10 minutes.

## What You'll Need

No special materials are needed.

## What to Do

Have participants get into a relaxed position, close their eyes, and breathe easily. Tell them that you're going to talk them through a perfect, stress-free day, and that, afterwards, they're going to use some feature of their fantasy to help improve their real day.

When participants are ready, talk them through a perfect day, as follows:

*You're in bed, extremely relaxed, and you're just*

*beginning to awaken on the morning of a perfect, stress-free day. This is a day when you're going to feel peaceful and fulfilled all day, morning 'til night.*

*Slowly, in your imagination, open your eyes.... Now look around.... What does the room look like? Is anyone with you? Gradually, easily, you get out of bed, wash up, and start your morning routine on this perfect, stress-free day. Where have you gone? Are you at work? Are you at home? Are people around you? Look around, slowly.... You feel at ease and at peace.... Where are you, and what are you doing?*

*It's lunch time now on this perfect, stress-free day. Look around, slowly.... Where are you having lunch, and with whom? Now it's afternoon, and you still feel at peace, like everything is right in the world. Where are you? What are you doing? Who, if anyone, is with you? Now dinner time has come.... Look around again.... Where are you having dinner, and what are you eating? Are you alone or with others?*

*It is the evening now of this perfect, peaceful, stress-free day.... How are you spending the evening hours? What's around you? Who's around you?*

*Finally, it's time for bed. You feel fulfilled and at peace.... You're in bed, and your eyes are closed, and you feel warm and heavy and serene.... Gradually, you fall asleep, reflecting gently about what you've seen and experienced during this perfect, stress-free day....*

Ask participants to open their eyes, and then ask some volunteers to report to the group about what their day was like. Finally, lead a brief discussion about the feasibility of making one's actual day more like the perfect one.

## Discussion Questions

1. How close is your fantasy day to your real day?
2. What features of your fantasy day could be transferred to your real day?
3. Did the "perfect day" fantasy teach you anything about yourself or give you any special insights into your life?

## If You Have More Time

Ask participants to list features of their perfect day that they might be able to incorporate into their real daily routine. For example, if they spent part of their perfect day gardening, could they bring some plants to work and then tend those plants? Ask some volunteers to tell the group what they've listed.

## Personal Touch

Put your image text on tape, perhaps with soothing music in the background, and play it to help you visualize the kind of day you'd *really* like to have.

# THE TIME-TESTED TEN COUNT

## In a Nutshell

Pairs of participants role-play situations in which one person is confrontational. The other person either responds immediately or after a slow ten-count. Participants switch roles, and a brief discussion follows.

## Time

15 minutes.

## What You'll Need

A blackboard or overhead projector might be useful.

## What to Do

Remind participants that intense emotional states subside quickly as time passes. The ten-count allows the arousal state to subside before we do something that we might easily regret later.

On a blackboard or screen, list a few work scenarios in

which one person is confrontational and another needs to respond.  Then pair off your participants and have them act out one of the scenarios in two different ways. The first time through, the  respondent replies to the attacker immediately.  The second time through, the respondent performs a slow, silent ten-count before responding.

Have them switch roles, pick another scenario, and repeat the exercise.

Finally, ask a few people to report on what happened in their role plays, and lead a brief discussion about the ten-count.

Here are a few scenarios you might use or adapt for this activity.   Add others to the list which are appropriate for the members of your group.

*Confrontations*

1)  Co-workers are discussing a particular project, and one accuses the other of not doing his or her share of the work.

2)  Someone who's been waiting a long time to use the photocopy machine accuses the person who's using the machine of hogging it.

3)  One person accuses the other of having spread false gossip about him or her at work.

## Discussion Questions

1. Does counting to ten actually work? When might it work well? When might it work poorly?
2. Do you presently use any techniques to get yourself to delay responding in conflict situations? If so, what techniques do you use?
3. What are some other methods you might use to delay your response to a hostile act?

## If You're Short on Time

Simply role-play a scenario with a volunteer from the group.

## Alternative

The ten-count is only one way to pause before acting. You might try variations on the procedure that use other methods of delaying a response. People can silently recite poems, adages, or Biblical passages, for example. Get suggestions from the group.

# TURN, TURN, TURN

## In a Nutshell

Participants turn and tilt their heads, following your instructions.

## Time

5 minutes.

## What You'll Need

No special materials are needed.

## What to Do

To begin, have participants sit in a relaxed position, breathe easily, and close their eyes. Now have people tilt and turn their heads as follows. Be sure to tell people not to force the movements. If someone's head will only tilt a few degrees without strain, that's fine.

1) Tilt the head forward slowly, downward toward the chest. Pause, count to three, then slowly bring the head back to the upright position. Repeat this three times.

2) Tilt the head back slowly (the nose will be pointing toward the ceiling). Pause, count to three, then slowly bring the head back to the upright position. Repeat this three times.

3) Tilt the head slowly to the right, toward the right shoulder. Pause, count to three, then slowly bring the head back to the upright position. Repeat this three times.

4) Tilt the head slowly to the left, toward the left shoulder. Pause, count to three, then slowly bring the head back to the upright position. Repeat this three times.

5) Tilt the head forward toward the chest, then slowly rotate the head upward toward the right shoulder, then toward the back (the nose will be pointing toward the ceiling), then downward toward the left shoulder, then forward toward the chest. Pause in this position and count to three, then repeat the circle two more times. Make each circle slow and continuous. Then repeat the cycle again, this time beginning each circle by rotating upward toward the left shoulder. Finally, bring the head back to the upright position.

## Discussion Questions

1. How does tilting and turning your head make you feel? Do you feel more relaxed?
2. In what setting would you feel comfortable doing

this exercise?  Where would you be reluctant to try it, and why?

## Tip!

Make sure that participants don't overextend their tilts in this exercise.  The purpose here is relaxation.

## Personal Touch

This is a great technique to do on your own.  If you'd like, you can even put it on tape and play the tape to help you stay calm.

# THE TURTLE TECHNIQUE

## In a Turtleshell

In a guided-imagery exercise, participants imagine themselves withdrawing into a cozy turtle shell, calming down, and then emerging to face the day.

## Time

5 minutes.

## What You'll Need

No special materials are required.

## What to Do

Have participants sit in a relaxed position, breathe easily, and close their eyes. Next, recite the following text:

> *The stressors are all around you—a supervisor making demands, customers complaining, and co-workers driving you crazy—and you need to get away. Fortunately, you've still got some primitive turtle genes hidden somewhere in the recesses of*

*your chromosomes, and now the time has come to turn those genes on. All around you, a great, green shell is forming. It's as beautiful and ornate as it is hard and impregnable. Slowly, you bring your head and arms and legs into that great shell. It's dark and warm and comfortable and comforting, this great shell. You feel secure and warm within its confines. The world around you is gone. You hear your breathing, and you feel calm and secure in the comforting darkness of your primitive home. You wait, and enjoy, and listen to the dark silence.... You are at peace....*

*Finally, you feel ready to emerge, back to the light. Slowly, gradually, you extend your arms and legs out into the world, and, finally, triumphantly, confidently, calmly, you extend your head back into reality. The stressors are there, but you feel refreshed, renewed, and in control.*

Have people open their eyes, and ask some volunteers how the exercise made them feel. Lead a brief discussion about the value of and possible applications of the technique.

## Discussion Questions

1. Do you ever feel the need to escape or withdraw while on the job? Please describe an occasion like this.
2. What do you do when you feel the need to escape or withdraw?

3. To what extent did the turtle image make you feel like you had withdrawn from the stressful setting?
4. Could you see yourself using the Turtle Technique in real situations? Why or why not? How might you see yourself using it?

## Personal Touch

As is true of all imagery techniques, this is a great technique to learn and practice on your own. Alligators all around? Head for the shell!

# THE TWENTY-EIGHT-HOUR DAY

## In a Nutshell

After reviewing some major principles of time management, participants complete Time-Management Plans (TMPs), with the goal of adding four new hours to the day.

## Time

30 minutes.

## What You'll Need

Writing materials for all participants, and copies of handout on page 175.

## What to Do

Review some major principles of time management. These techniques are summarized on page 175, which you may want to display.

Now, have participants spend 15 minutes writing out a personal Time-Management Plan (TMP). Next to each technique, have people estimate the amount of time they would save per day if they used that technique. The goal is to shave *four hours* off of the day—about half of the traditional work day. Ask people for their totals. Ask where they had the most savings, whether the plan is feasible, and so on. You may want to compute a grand total on a blackboard or screen.

## Discussion Questions

1. How would better time management help you reduce stress?
2. What are the impediments to better time management in your life? How can you defeat them?
3. How much time would you save with better time management?

## Personal Touch

No group? Not to worry. Create your own TMP and devise ways to shave off those minutes.

# MANAGING TIME

- DELEGATE
- USE TECHNOLOGY WISELY
- USE COMMUTING TIME WISELY
- REDUCE MEETING TIME

- REDUCE INTERRUPTIONS
- REDUCE  DISTRACTIONS
- CONTROL  PAPERWORK
- SCHEDULE WISELY
- SCHEDULE LEISURE TIME

- SCHEDULE SCHEDULING TIME
- SCHEDULE PLANNING TIME
- PRIORITIZE
- KEEP A TIME LOG
- PLAN
- USE PLANNERS

- USE PLANNING SOFTWARE
- FILE EFFICIENTLY
- CONTROL APPOINTMENTS
- MANAGE YOUR WRITING

# THE WARMTH OF THE SUN

## In a Nutshell

Participants sit in a relaxed position, close their eyes, and listen to you describing a relaxing scene at an idyllic beach.

## Time

10 minutes.

## What You'll Need

No special materials are needed.

## What to Do

Have participants get into a relaxed position. Then, in a soothing voice, recite the following:

*Listen closely, very closely, to my voice.... Feel your body relax and the sounds and sensations of this room gradually disappear.... Focus, concentrate on my voice and the feeling of relaxation that's beginning to grow in your body.... That's good.... Keep relaxing.... Breathe slowly and easily....*

*Around you now an image is beginning to form. It's dim at first. With your eyes still closed, and your body relaxed, slowly become aware of the sensations that surround you.... A beautiful scene is beginning to emerge.... You're laying on your back on warm, white sand.... Focus on the warmth of the sand on the back side of your body as the scene begins to form around you.... You can feel the warm sand on the back sides of your legs, on your buttocks, on the small of your back, on your upper-back, and on the back sides of your arms..... Feel the warmth, soothing you, penetrating the skin on the back side of your body.... Above you is a bright, azure blue sky, unblemished by the smallest cloud. The sun, large and yellow and alive, is nearly straight above you in the sky. You can feel its heat radiating down toward your body, enveloping you, cradling you, cuddling you, in soothing tendrils of warmth. Focus on the warmth of the sun as it penetrates the skin of your face... of your neck... of your torso... of your arms... of your legs.... Envision the tendrils of light and heat connecting you to the glowing ball in the sky.... Let the warmth of the sun relax you, envelop you, hold you, and bring you peace.... Now focus on the warmth of the sand beneath you, so that your whole body is wrapped in a soothing warmth.... You don't feel hot. You're not perspiring. You're just comforted in the soothing warmth that surrounds you.*

*In the distance, you hear the gentle sounds of*

*ocean waves, but you don't see the ocean. You hear the gentle rush, rush, rush, of the waves.... You feel the warmth of the sun above and the warmth of the sand beneath you.... You hear the gentle beating of the waves, and you feel relaxed and at peace....*

*Above you, wisps of air gently caress your warm skin, teasing the hairs on your skin, soothing you and bringing you peace. In the distance, you think you hear the rustle of tall grasses, but you can't see them. You see the sun and sky.... You feel the warmth of the sun, the caress of the gentle breeze on your skin, and the soothing support of the white sand beneath you.... You hear the rush, rush, rush of the ocean's waves.... You feel a deep, soothing peace....*

*Now, gradually, very gradually, open your eyes, and return to the present.*

## Discussion Questions

1. Did the feeling of warmth and relaxation persist after I asked you to open your eyes? Is the feeling persisting now? How do you feel right now?
2. How might you use this technique in the workplace? At home? How might you use a taped version of this exercise?
3. What might prevent you from using this technique in the workplace? How can you get around these difficulties?

## Alternative

You may want to create a more intense experience by playing a tape of soothing music or ocean sounds. You can also dim the room lights to minimize distractions.

## Personal Touch

Grab a copy of the tape for yourself, and head for the beach (in your imagination, anyway).

# WHAT D'YA KNOW?

## In a Nutshell

Participants take a short quiz on stress-management and relaxation, and then, with the leader's guidance, self-score the quiz and discuss the results.

## Time

30 minutes.

## What You'll Need

Copies of handouts on pages 184 and 185 should be distributed.

## What to Do

Distribute copies of the handout on page 184, answer questions people might have about the test, and have people complete it. This should take between five and ten minutes. Then distribute copies of page 185 and have people self-score the tests. The latter will allow people to generate an overall score, as well as sub-scores in four competency categories, which include:

1) *Manages or reduces sources of stress*
2) *Practices relaxation techniques*
3) *Manages his or her thoughts*
4) *Plans and analyzes to minimize stress*

Lead a brief discussion about what these categories mean and how participants might get additional training to sharpen their skills.

# Discussion Questions

1. Where are you especially skillful in managing stress? Where could you use some improvement?
2. What additional training do you feel you'd like to have to help you improve your stress-management skills?
3. Were you surprised by the results of the quiz? How so?

# If You're Short on Time

Administer the test orally, having people record their answers on a blank sheet of paper, and then talk them through the scoring.

# Tip!

Be sure to indicate that this quiz does not measure the participants' current level of stress but that it focuses on their current abilities to fight stress.

## Personal Touch

For your own benefit, or to make yourself a more effective leader, be sure to take and score the stress-management quiz in this chapter. Where are *your* strengths and weaknesses as a stress manager? How might you improve your skills and practices?

# EPSTEIN STRESS-MANAGEMENT INVENTORY
## for Individuals (ESMI-i) [Abridged]

*Please use a pencil to fill in the bubble that best represents your reaction to each of the statements below.*

1. I have constructive outlets for my aggression.　　　　Agree ① ② ③ ④ ⑤ Disagree
2. I frequently visualize soothing scenes in order to relax.　Agree ① ② ③ ④ ⑤ Disagree
3. Breathing is a very hard thing to control.　　　　　Agree ① ② ③ ④ ⑤ Disagree
4. I'm aware that some of my beliefs are probably irrational.　Agree ① ② ③ ④ ⑤ Disagree
5. I keep an up-to-date list of things I'm supposed to do.　Agree ① ② ③ ④ ⑤ Disagree
6. I always spend a few minutes each morning planning my day.　Agree ① ② ③ ④ ⑤ Disagree
7. I keep an up-to-date list of things I love to do.　　Agree ① ② ③ ④ ⑤ Disagree
8. I try to avoid destructive ways of dealing with stress.　Agree ① ② ③ ④ ⑤ Disagree
9. I frequently manipulate my environment to improve my mood.　Agree ① ② ③ ④ ⑤ Disagree
10. I try to make sure that my meetings end early or on time.　Agree ① ② ③ ④ ⑤ Disagree
11. A computer can be a great tool for relieving stress.　Agree ① ② ③ ④ ⑤ Disagree
12. I have trouble prioritizing.　　　　　　　　　Agree ① ② ③ ④ ⑤ Disagree
13. I'm comfortable asking other people for help.　　Agree ① ② ③ ④ ⑤ Disagree
14. I very rarely stretch my body.　　　　　　　Agree ① ② ③ ④ ⑤ Disagree
15. I regularly tense and relax my muscles as a way of relaxing.　Agree ① ② ③ ④ ⑤ Disagree
16. I wish I got more exercise.　　　　　　　　Agree ① ② ③ ④ ⑤ Disagree
17. I try to fight stress before it starts.　　　　　Agree ① ② ③ ④ ⑤ Disagree
18. I try to keep my desk clear of junk.　　　　　Agree ① ② ③ ④ ⑤ Disagree
19. I have trouble delegating.　　　　　　　　　Agree ① ② ③ ④ ⑤ Disagree
20. I sit and stand in special ways to help me stay relaxed.　Agree ① ② ③ ④ ⑤ Disagree
21. Distractions are inevitable during the work day.　Agree ① ② ③ ④ ⑤ Disagree
22. My calendar isn't always available when I need it.　Agree ① ② ③ ④ ⑤ Disagree
23. I frequently use special breathing techniques to help me relax.　Agree ① ② ③ ④ ⑤ Disagree
24. I waste time trying to find misplaced files and documents.　Agree ① ② ③ ④ ⑤ Disagree
25. I frequently post reminder notes to keep myself on track.　Agree ① ② ③ ④ ⑤ Disagree
26. I regularly use massage or self-massage to help me relax.　Agree ① ② ③ ④ ⑤ Disagree
27. I often try to use humor to diffuse tension.　　Agree ① ② ③ ④ ⑤ Disagree
28. I regularly examine and try to correct my irrational beliefs.　Agree ① ② ③ ④ ⑤ Disagree

**184**

# Self-Scorer for ESMI-i [Abridged]

*To score your test: Generate your total score by listing a 1 or a 0 in the blanks in the left-hand column below. Give yourself a 1 if you filled in a bubble in the shaded areas; otherwise give yourself a 0. Count up the 1's and fill in your total score at the bottom of the column. The highest possible score is a 28. If you scored lower than that, you can probably improve your stress-management practices. To focus on specific competencies, complete the four boxes below by circling item numbers for which you received a score of 1. In each box, count the 1's, and fill in the blank with the total. If you scored below the maximum, you may need to strengthen your skills within that competency area.*

1. ❶ ❷ ③ ④ ⑤___
2. ❶ ❷ ③ ④ ⑤___
3. ① ② ③ ❹ ❺___
4. ❶ ❷ ③ ④ ⑤___
5. ❶ ❷ ③ ④ ⑤___
6. ❶ ❷ ③ ④ ⑤___
7. ❶ ❷ ③ ④ ⑤___
8. ❶ ❷ ③ ④ ⑤___
9. ❶ ❷ ③ ④ ⑤___
10. ❶ ❷ ③ ④ ⑤___
11. ❶ ❷ ③ ④ ⑤___
12. ① ② ③ ❹ ❺___
13. ❶ ❷ ③ ④ ⑤___
14. ① ② ③ ❹ ❺___
15. ❶ ❷ ③ ④ ⑤___
16. ① ② ③ ❹ ❺___
17. ❶ ❷ ③ ④ ⑤___
18. ❶ ❷ ③ ④ ⑤___
19. ① ② ③ ❹ ❺___
20. ❶ ❷ ③ ④ ⑤___
21. ① ② ③ ❹ ❺___
22. ① ② ③ ❹ ❺___
23. ❶ ❷ ③ ④ ⑤___
24. ① ② ③ ❹ ❺___
25. ❶ ❷ ③ ④ ⑤___
26. ❶ ❷ ③ ④ ⑤___
27. ❶ ❷ ③ ④ ⑤___
28. ❶ ❷ ③ ④ ⑤___

TOTAL SCORE_____

---

**1) *Manages or reduces sources of stress*.** You routinely manage or reduce sources of stress, both real and possible, in your life.

| 6 | 9 | 10 | 11 | 12 | 13 |
|---|---|----|----|----|----|
| 18 | 19 | 21 | 22 | 24 | |

*Total 1's: ____ / 11*

---

**2) *Practices relaxation techniques.*** You regularly practice a variety of relaxation techniques to prevent or relieve stress.

| 1 | 2 | 3 | 14 | 15 |
|---|---|---|----|----|
| 16 | 20 | 23 | 26 | |

*Total 1's: ____ / 9*

---

**3) *Manages his or her thoughts.*** You manage your thoughts in order to reduce the likelihood that you will perceive events as threatening.

| 4 | 27 | 28 |
|---|----|----|

*Total 1's:____ / 3*

---

**4) *Plans and analyzes to minimize stress.*** You practice self-management techniques, avoid destructive methods of stress management, and take a proactive approach to stress management.

| 5 | 7 | 8 | 17 | 25 |
|---|---|---|----|----|

*Total 1's:____ / 5*

©2000, Dr. Robert Epstein.

**185**

# THE WHOOSH GAME

## In a Nutshell

Participants envision hostile speech turning into alphabet letters and "whooshing" by their heads.

## Time

10-15 minutes.

## What You'll Need

No special materials or supplies are required.

## What to Do

Ask the members of your group to help you compose a short list of people—the Hostile People list—who might speak harshly to them in the workplace. The list will vary with the workplace, of course, but you may get suggestions like: *angry customer, critical boss, inconsiderate co-worker,* and so on.

Now ask for a volunteer to play the part of one of the hostile people on the list. Have the person come to the front of the room and await further instructions. Then explain to the group:

*Our volunteer is going to speak harshly to you for the next minute or two, acting out the role of [name of role here]. To minimize the impact of the harsh words, I want you to visualize these words turning into their spelled-out forms as they emerge from the volunteer's mouth. In other words, I want you to visualize a stream of alphabet letters heading in your direction, coming from the volunteer's mouth. As the words fly toward you, I want you to visualize them whooshing by your head on one side or the other. If it helps you to create this image, you can move your hand like this [move the flat of your hand quickly from the front to the back of the head so that some air whooshes by your ear]. You can still listen to the words—in other words, you're not trying to ignore the speaker—but you are trying to minimize the emotional impact of the words.*

Answer any questions that people might have about the technique, and then have the volunteer start the hostile monologue. When it's done, have a few people from the audience tell you what impact, if any, the whooshing had on their reaction to the abusive language.

If time allows, repeat the procedure with one or two more volunteers, each assuming different roles selected from the Hostile People List. Complete the exercise with a brief discussion about the *whoosh* technique and its possible applications.

## Discussion Questions

1. Did *whooshing* minimize the impact of the hostile language you heard? Why do you think it worked (or didn't work)?
2. How might you use the *whoosh* technique in the workplace?
3. How is *whooshing* different from ignoring?

## If You Have More Time

You can expand the exercise by first having people listen to a hostile presenter (or to a tape) *without whooshing* and then having them listen to the same presenter (or tape) *with whooshing.* You can jazz up your presentation by playing a tape of real wind whooshing through trees or canyons.

## Tip!

Remember, *whooshing* is not the same as ignoring. Ignoring an angry customer will only make the customer more angry. When you *whoosh* the customer's words, your goal is to respond calmly to the customer's needs, without succumbing to the emotional impact of the words.

## Personal Touch

Practice "whooshing" in front of a mirror. Then give it a try with a friend—or with someone not so friendly.

# WITHIN YOU, WITHOUT YOU

## In a Nutshell

With their eyes closed, participants learn to shift their focus repeatedly from internal to external sensations.

## Time

10 minutes.

## What You'll Need

No special materials or supplies are required.

## What to Do

Ask participants to get into a relaxed position and close their eyes. Then, in a soothing tone, recite the following:

*Focus closely, very closely, on my voice.... Relax your body, breathe easily, and stay focused on my voice.... I'm going to ask you to look into your body, and then to look outside your body, in a way that you don't normally do. Listen carefully to my instructions, continue to breathe easily, and follow my instructions as best you can.... First, I want you to look inside your body. We'll start with your head. Turn your focus to the inside of your head.... It's dark in there, isn't it? Look all around the inside of your head. Explore your brain... the back side of your eyes... the inside of your eyes... the inside of your ears... the inside of your nose... your mouth... your tongue... your chin.... Watch your blood flow and your muscles twitch.... Watch your neurons fire.... Feel your eyeballs move in their sockets.... Look around again, slowly, all through your head....*

*Now shift your focus to your neck and shoulders.... Feel the tension in your tendons and muscles.... Explore the inside of your neck and throat.... Look inside your left shoulder... and then your right shoulder. Feel the way your neck is connected to your head... and to your torso.... Listen to the blood flow.... Look again, all around the inside of your neck and shoulders....*

*Now shift your focus to your torso.... Look all around at the inside of your torso... at your ribs... your heart... your lungs... Listen to the majesty of your heart beat.... Watch the blood flow, in soft, easy pulses, from one chamber of the heart to another... through the arteries out to the rest of your torso.... Imagine yourself flowing with the blood, nourishing the cells along the way.... Listen again, to your heart beat. Watch the heart, expanding and contracting inside your chest, pumping the blood into your arteries.... Look all around the inside of your torso....   Watch, listen, marvel....*

*Look around again all through the inside of your body, moving from your head... to your neck and shoulders... to your torso... to your lower body... to your feet... to your arms... to your hands.... to your finger tips....   And relax, and breathe easily... Now let's look at the outside of the body, at the sensations we feel at the surface of our body, moving slowly from top to bottom.... Let's start at the scalp.   Focus on the top of the head, at the sensations on the skin of the scalp....   Feel the tingling of the hair and the air above the scalp. Shift the focus to the back of the head... to the sides.... to the ears.... Listen to the air caressing the tiny hairs on the skin of your ears... your nose... the tip of your chin....*

*Now let's shift our focus to the upper body.  Feel the cloth of your shirt or blouse touching your left arm... your shoulder... your chest... your right arm... your upper back... your abdomen... your lower back....   Feel the hairs on your skin bending against the weight of the cloth. Let your skin begin to tingle as you focus on the contours and textures of the cloth....*

*Move your focus, very slowly, all around the immediate exterior of your body, feeling the textures, and the pressures, and the sounds, and the lights, and the temperatures....*

*Now slowly, gradually, open your eyes, and return your attention to the room around you....*

If time allows, have people shift their focus, several times if possible, from the inside to the outside of the body. With each shift, you can describe fewer details, leaving the exploration to the participant.

## Discussion Questions

1. When you explored the outside of your body, did you feel any tingling? Could you feel pressures and textures and temperatures? What, specifically, did you sense that you would not normally sense?
2. Did this exercise take you away from this room? Did it take you away from your usual train of thinking? Did it relax you? Why or why not?
3. How might you apply this exercise in your everyday routine? What value might it serve?

## Personal Touch

You may want to put this image text on tape. A musical background would probably be too distracting for this one, though.

# THE WORLD IS ROUND

## In a Nutshell

Participants learn that their perspective on a stressful situation—the way they think about it—can determine whether or not they will feel stress.

## Time

10 minutes.

## What You'll Need

No materials are needed.

## What to Do

Tell the participants that you are going to tell them a story. Then recite the following:

*It's Medieval times somewhere on the southern coast of Italy. A man is standing on a dock, there to see his friends and family leave on a large sailing ship. The sky is blue, the winds are steady from the east, and the sea is calm. The ship is at the dock, and all of his loved ones are on* board—his devoted wife, his three children, his youthful parents, his brother and sister, and his closest friends. They're all waving to him from the deck high above where he's standing. He waves back. The man is feeling a little sad about the impending departure, but he's also excited for his loved ones. In general, he's feeling pretty good. After all, it's a beautiful day, the sea is calm and the wind is steady, and his loved ones are happy and safe. In a few days, they'll be settled near some fertile land in a distant valley, where he will join them in a few months.

The captain shouts the order to set sail, deck hands release the ship from the dock, and the ship begins to move away. The man continues to wave, and he shouts his last goodbyes. The voices of his loved ones mingle with the shouts of the crew, as the ship moves farther and farther from the dock, away from the shore, toward the endless ocean.

As the ship moves farther and farther away, the man feels a bit sad, already missing his friends and family, but he's not especially upset. The ship moves farther and farther out to sea, and, because the air is so clear, he can continue to see the ship as it moves toward the distant horizon. When it reaches the horizon, the man suddenly feels quite ill, because he sees the ship starting to sink. He can clearly see the ocean swallowing the ship, first the hull and the deck, and finally, the masts and the sails. He imagines his dear children, his wife, *his friends and parents, all drowning, horribly, as the ship disappears beneath the water. He collapses to the ground and cries out in despair. He tears at his clothes and his hair. He pounds the wooden dock beneath him with his fists. He has lost everything.*

*But the ship and all his loved ones are actually fine. The man believes the ship has sunk because—this being Medieval times—he believes the world is flat. He has seen, with his own eyes, the ship sink into the water and disappear from view. In a flat world, this can mean only one thing: The ship was lost and all aboard have died.*

*But how would the story end if, the day before, we had taught this man that the world is round? There he is, on the same dock, near the same ship, with all his loved ones aboard. The ship moves out to sea, and he feels fine. The ship reaches the horizon and disappears—and he still feels fine. The situation is <u>exactly the same</u>—same ship, same dock, same images. But he's <u>interpreting</u> what he sees differently. When he believed that the world was flat, he <u>interpreted</u> what he saw in a way that induced a state of utter despair. Now that he knows that the world is round, he attaches a <u>different interpretation</u> to what he sees, and he feels fine.*

At this point, lead a discussion about the meaning and applicability of the story.

# Discussion Questions

1. Can you give an example of a situation that you always interpret negatively? Of a situation that you always interpret positively?
2. Describe a situation that you usually see in negative terms, and tell us you might reinterpret that situation in positive terms?
3. Having heard the story about the Medieval man, what does the phrase, "The World Is Round," mean to you? How might you apply this concept to your life? To your work situation?

# If You Have More Time

Divide the group into teams of between three and five people, and distribute blank paper to all participants. Have each team develop three potentially stressful work scenarios and then sketch out a negative interpretation and then a positive interpretation for each of the scenarios. Give the teams 15 minutes to complete this process, and then have representatives from some of the teams present one of the team's scenarios, along with the negative and then the positive interpretations. Lead a brief discussion about the results.

# Tip!

"The World Is Round" shows dramatically that our stress reactions depend to a great extent on our beliefs and knowledge.  And it's also a great story because the world *is* actually round.   Remember that the next time your world seems out of shape.

# INDEX

# ABOUT THE AUTHOR

One of the world's leading experts on human behavior, ROBERT EPSTEIN is Editor-in-Chief of *Psychology Today* magazine and host of the magazine's nationally syndicated radio program. Dr. Epstein is also University Research Professor at United States International University in San Diego, Chairman and CEO of InnoGen International, and Director Emeritus of the Cambridge Center for Behavioral Studies in Massachusetts. He received his Ph.D. in psychology in 1981 from Harvard University. He is the developer of Generativity Theory, a scientific theory of the creative process, and a contributor to the *Encyclopedia of Creativity*. His research on creativity and problem solving has been reported in *Time* magazine, the *New York Times*, and *Discover*, as well as on national and international radio and television. Epstein's recent books include *Stress-Management and Relaxation Activities for Trainers* (McGraw-Hill), *The New Psychology Today Reader* (Kendall/Hunt), Creativity *Games for Trainers* (McGraw-Hill), *Cognition, Creativity, and Behavior: Selected Essays* (Praeger), *Pure Fitness: Body Meets Mind* (Masters Press, with Lori "Ice" Fetrick of "The American Gladiators"), *Self-Help Without the Hype* (Performance Management Publications), and *Irrelativity* (Astrion). He is also the editor of two books of writings by the eminent psychologist, B. F. Skinner, with whom Epstein collaborated at Harvard. He has served on the faculties of Boston University, the University of Massachusetts at Amherst, the University of California San Diego, and other universities. He served as Professor of Psychology and Chair of the Department of Psychology at National University and was also appointed Research Professor there. He is also Adjunct Professor of Psychology at San Diego State University. Dr. Epstein directed the Loebner Prize Competition in Artificial Intelligence for five years and has done consulting and training for businesses and mental health programs for more than fifteen years. He has been a commentator for NPR's "Marketplace" and the Voice of America, and his popular writings have appeared in *Reader's Digest*, *The Washington Post*, *Psychology Today*, *Good Housekeeping*, *Parenting*, and other magazines and newspapers. Dr. Epstein can be reached by email at repstein@post.harvard.edu.